Intimate
Violence
in
Families

To the memory of
Barry A. Marks

Intimate Violence

in

Families

Third Edition

Richard J. Gelles

SAGE Publications
International Educational and Professional Publisher
Thousand Oaks   London   New Delhi

362.8292
6318;
1997

For information address:

SAGE Publications, Inc.
2455 Teller Road
Thousand Oaks, California 91320
E-mail: order@sagepub.com

SAGE Publications Ltd.
6 Bonhill Street
London EC2A 4PU
United Kingdom

SAGE Publications India Pvt. Ltd.
M-32 Market
Greater Kailash I
New Delhi 110 048 India

Printed in the United States of America

Library of Congress Cataloging-in-Publication Data

Gelles, Richard J.
    Intimate violence in families / Richard J. Gelles. — 3rd ed.
        p.   cm.
    Includes bibliographical references (p.   ) and index.
    ISBN 0-7619-0122-1 (cloth: acid-free paper). — ISBN 0-7619-0123-X (pbk.: acid-free paper)
    1. Family violence—United States.   I. Title.
HV6626.2.GH45   1997
362.82′92—dc20   96-35646

04 05 06 07 08 12 11 10 9 8

Acquiring Editor:	Margaret Zusky
Editorial Assistant:	Renée Piernot
Production Editor:	Diana E. Axelsen
Production Assistant:	Karen Wiley
Typesetter/Designer:	Janelle LeMaster
Indexer:	Trish Wittenstein
Cover Designer:	Candice Harman
Print Buyer:	Anna Chin

CONTENTS

ACKNOWLEDGMENTS

This book owes much to my previous work and writings on family and intimate violence. A number of colleagues and friends have been particularly helpful over the years and have assisted in considering the difficult, complex, and often emotional issues surrounding intimate and family violence. Claire Pedrick Cornell was my coauthor for the first two editions of this book and has now moved on with her life and family. Murray Straus has been a teacher, mentor, colleague, and friend for the past 25 years. Eli and Carolyn Newberger have also been colleagues and friends for more than 20 years and were responsible for showing me the link between research and clinical practice. They changed how I look at and study intimate violence.

The University of Rhode Island Family Violence Research Program has been a source of support, guidance, and inspiration for the past 6 years. Glenn Wolfner, Deborah Levesque, Heidi Reckseik, Lisa Jones, Amy Silverman, Joseph Youngblood, Christine Harkins, and Deborah DeBare are the former and current members of the Family Violence Research Program who, even though they didn't always know it, helped me with this book. Jody Brown, Associate Director of the Family Violence Research Program, reviewed drafts of this book and made many important suggestions for changes and revisions.

My two sons, Jason (22) and David (19), watched me write the first two editions of this book. They have now moved on with their lives and were away at college while I wrote this edition. The house was lonelier and the work went slower without them at home. My wife, Judy, continues to provide critical social and emotional support.

1

INTRODUCTION

People are more likely to be killed, physically assaulted, hit, beat up, slapped, or spanked in their own homes by other family members than anywhere else, or by anyone else, in our society. Not only is this true today, it is true throughout the history of the United States. This statement applies not only to American families, but it is also an accurate assessment of family life in England, Western Europe, and many other countries and societies around the globe.

We do not commonly think of the family as society's most violent social institution. Typically, family life is thought to be warm, intimate, stress reducing, and the place that people flee to for safety. Our desire to idealize family life is partly responsible for a tendency either not to see family and intimate violence or to condone it as being a necessary and important part of raising children, relating to spouses, and conducting other family transactions.

This book is designed to provide a basic overview of the subject of family and intimate violence. Many books take a look at only one aspect of violence and maltreatment in the home. Typically, a writer will discuss child abuse, sexual abuse, wife abuse, or elder abuse, but very rarely do books and articles attempt to examine all aspects of violence in families and try to look at the whole picture of family and intimate violence.

Although it is important to understand the nature and causes of child abuse or wife abuse, concentrating on just one form of violence or abuse may obscure the entire picture and hinder a more complete understanding of the causes and consequences of abuse.

A case example of the problems produced by narrowly focusing on just one type of abuse is illustrated by the experience of a hospital emergency room staff. The physicians and nurses in the inner-city emergency room had treated a women on three occasions. The woman had arrived in the emergency room suffering from a variety of bruises and abrasions. Each time, she had been carefully interviewed by a nurse or social worker, and each time she had admitted that her live-in boyfriend had beaten her and inflicted the injuries. The emergency room staff treated the injuries, x-rayed the woman to see if any bones had been broken, and provided her—on all three occasions—with information about shelters and services for battered women. However, on no occasion was any notice taken of the 2-year-old child who had accompanied the woman. The little boy either slept or played quietly with the few toys that were in the emergency room waiting area. No doctor, nurse, or social worker had asked the woman about her son, no one had examined the boy, and apparently, no one had considered that either the boyfriend or the mother might possibly be maltreating the little boy. The emergency room staff focused exclusively on the problem of woman battering. A month after the mother's third emergency room visit, her 2-year-old son arrived in the emergency room unconscious— beaten nearly to death by the live-in boyfriend, who used a broom handle to assault the little child.

This case illustrates dramatically that one form of family violence may be closely connected to other acts of violence in the home. To focus on just one type of family violence often causes one to miss the overall picture. I also believe that one can only understand, explain, treat, and prevent family and intimate violence by understanding the operation and function of the entire family system.

Myths and Controversies That Hinder
Understanding of Family and Intimate Violence

How is it possible that families have been violent for centuries, all over the globe, yet we have only recently discovered and attended to family violence as a serious family and social problem? How is it that after 30 years of intensive research and practice in this field, we can still read newspaper accounts that talk about instances where children who were identified by social service agencies as abused, and whose cases have been followed by social workers for months, are killed, virtually under the nose of the person who was supposed to protect them? One answer to these two questions is that there are a number of myths and controversies about family violence that tend to hinder both public recognition and effective professional practice.

This book is designed to explode many of the conventional myths about family violence and replace these myths with knowledge derived from scholarly research. In addition, the book also explores some of the major controversies in the study and treatment of family and intimate violence. As a preview of the issues that will be taken up, and as a means of focusing on some of the more popular and persistent myths, this section presents the major myths and controversies hindering our understanding of family violence.

1. Family and intimate violence is a significant social and public
health problem but not an inevitable aspect of family relations.

Until the 1960s, most people considered family violence a rare phenomenon. What few official statistics there were tended to bear out this assumption. Few states required professionals or public agencies to report known or suspected instances of child abuse. When David Gil (1970) surveyed the entire country in 1967 to determine how many valid cases of physical child abuse there were, he found about 6,000. The individual state definitions of abuse and the procedures used to investigate reports of child abuse influenced the total number reported. California had more than 3,500 reports; Rhode Island had none. Until recently, there were few localities or states that required reporting of domestic violence or adult abuse. Today, at least seven states have laws that specifically address the issue of reporting when domestic violence or adult abuse is suspected (Hyman, 1995). Prior to 1970, few hospitals bothered to categorize women patients they treated as either abused or nonabused. Police departments did keep records of how many domestic disturbance calls they received and investigated, but many times the records were inaccurate or incomplete. Sometimes a husband assaulting his wife would be recorded as a domestic disturbance, and other times it would be recorded as an assault.

The strong belief that families are places people turn *to* for help, and the perception that city streets hold the greatest risk for women and children, helped to continue the myth of the rareness of family violence even into the 1990s. As different types of family violence are discovered and examined, most people find it difficult to believe how many individuals and families are involved in violence in the home.

There has been no shortage of publicity about family violence in the 1990s. Public awareness about child abuse, sexual abuse, wife abuse, and elder abuse has been fueled by a combination of public awareness campaigns designed to educate the public about the dangers and costs of family violence and high-profile cases of family violence. Public discussion of and attention to family violence has included the sensational case of Lorena Bobbitt, who cut off her husband's penis after he allegedly raped her; the double murder of their parents by the Menendez brothers in California; self-disclosures of their own abuse victimization by celebrities such as Oprah Winfrey and former Miss America Carolyn Sapp; a nearly daily discussion of various forms and types of abuse on daytime television talk shows; and finally, the killing of Nicole Brown Simpson and Ronald Goldman and the trial and acquittal of O.J. Simpson.

The public awareness campaigns and the publicity attendant to the high-profile cases of family violence tend to be accompanied by claims of an "epidemic" of family violence, a rising tide of family violence, and the emergence of various "factoids" used to highlight the claim that family violence is growing, widespread, and harmful.

In the wake of the killings of Nicole Brown Simpson and Ronald Goldman and the allegation that the killer was Nicole Brown Simpson's former husband, O.J., there were a number of statistics that were repeated over and over about the extent of spouse abuse. Among the three most widely repeated "facts" were the following:

> More women are treated in emergency rooms for battering injuries than for muggings, rapes, and traffic accidents combined.

> Family violence has killed as many women in the past 5 years as the total number of Americans who were killed in the Vietnam War.

The March of Dimes reports that battering during pregnancy is the leading cause of birth defects and infant mortality.

Not only were these widely repeated, they were attributed to "authoritative sources." For example, the first "fact" about emergency room visits was attributed to the Centers for Disease Control and former Surgeon Generals C. Everett Koop and Antonia Novello. The Centers for Disease Control has repeatedly backed away from being the source of this "fact," stating that it is actually based on a very small study of a single emergency room. Even the authors of that study were tentative about the proportion of women who seek emergency room treatment who are battered. The authors' actual conclusion was that battering *may* (emphasis added) be the single most common source of serious injury to women, accounting for more injury than auto accidents, muggings, and rape combined (Stark et al., 1981).

The second "fact" is attributed to Robert McAfee, the former president of the American Medical Association. The "fact" is not accurate, because, as reported in Chapter 4, approximately 1,500 women are killed each year by husbands or boyfriends, for a total of 7,500 in 5 years, whereas there were 50,000 American causalities in the Vietnam War.

Finally, the March of Dimes reports no study of theirs or any other reputable researcher that finds the results attributed to the March of Dimes in the above "fact."

These are but a few of what some call "advocacy" statistics in the area of family violence (see, e.g., Sommers, 1994). The statistics and quotes are not put forward with malevolent intent or to deliberately deceive people. They are cited and cited again in an attempt to focus public and policy attention on the problem of family violence. Unfortunately, inaccurate statistics can obscure the true nature of the problem. Moreover, some of those who oppose efforts to deal with family violence can undermine advocates' claims for resources and new public policies by demonstrating that the so-called facts are inaccurate.

Family and intimate violence is indeed a significant social and public health problem. It is not, however, an inevitable aspect of family relations. Although there are millions of victims of family violence each year and thousands of fatalities, severe instances of family violence that result in injury are still relatively low-base-rate behaviors that vary across groups and cultures.

2. Family violence is confined to mentally disturbed or sick people.

A woman drowns her twin 6-month-old daughters. Another mother throws her daughter off a bridge into icy water. A mother and father plunge their 4-year-old into a bathtub filled with boiling water. A father has sexual intercourse with his 6-month-old daughter. A woman waits for her husband to take a shower, then fires a bullet into his skull at close range with a .357 magnum. These descriptions, and accompanying color slides of the harm done to the victims, are usually enough to convince most people that only someone who is mentally disturbed or truly psychotic would inflict such grievous harm onto a defenseless child, woman, or man. One way of upholding the image of the nurturant and safe family is to combine the notion that family violence is rare with the myth that only "sick" people abuse family members. Combining the two assumptions allows us to believe that when and if violence does take place, it is the problem of "people other than us."

The manner by which people determine that abusers are sick undermines the claim of mental illness. "People who abuse women and children are sick," we are told. How do you know they are sick? "Because they abuse women and children." This explanation does nothing more than substitute the word *sick* for *abuse*. The key question is, without knowing what someone did to his or her spouse or child, could you accurately diagnose him or her as mentally ill? In most cases, this is impossible. The sociologist Murray Straus (1980) claims that fewer than 10% of all instances of family violence are caused by mental illness or psychiatric disorders.

3. Family violence is confined to the lower class.

One of the consequences of the massive publicity generated by the murder of Nicole Brown Simpson and the trial of her ex-husband, O.J. Simpson, was a focus on violence in affluent families. Although there is increased awareness about the extent of family violence and the fact that violence is not always caused by mental illness or psychopathology, many people still believe that violence in general, and family violence in particular, is confined to lower-class families and the families of racial and ethnic minorities. There was a small sensation produced in the week following the murder of Nicole Brown Simpson when *Newsweek* magazine ran an unretouched police mug shot of O.J. Simpson while *Time* magazine ran an artist's rendition of the same photograph. The *Time* picture portrayed O.J. Simpson with much darker skin, almost as if the purpose of the drawing was to portray O.J. Simpson closer to the public stereotype of the lower-class, minority abuser.

Next to the myth of mental illness, the next most pervasive myth about family violence is that it is confined to the lower class. Like all myths, there is a grain of truth behind this belief. Researchers do find more *reported* violence and abuse among the lower class. For example, in the Second National Family Violence Survey, the rate of abusive violence toward women in households with total incomes below $10,000 per year was about 70 per 1,000, whereas the rate in households with total incomes more than $40,000 per year was a little less than 20 per 1,000 (Gelles, 1992, 1995). Official reports of child abuse indicate an overwhelming overrepresentation of lower-class families being reported as abusers. However, by virtue of being in the lower class, families run a greater risk of being correctly *and falsely* labeled abusers if their children are seen with injuries (Newberger, Reed, Daniel, Hyde, & Kotelchuck, 1977). Believing that abuse of wives and children is confined to the lower class is yet another way people try to see acts of others as deviant and their own behavior as normal.

4. Family violence occurs in all groups—social factors are not relevant.

When the first medical practitioners began to notice and attend to cases of child abuse, one of the first things they were struck by was that the children came from every type of social, racial, economic, and age group. Those who work with battered women also point out that women of all cultures, races, occupations, and income levels are battered.

Indeed, offenders and victims of family violence come from every level of society. It is also true that most forms of family and intimate violence do not occur with equal frequency across social groups. Social factors are relevant in explaining family violence.

For a factor to be a cause of family violence does not mean that it has to be perfectly associated with abuse. For poverty to be a causal factor it is not necessary that only poor people abuse wives, children, or parents and that no well-to-do people are abusive. There are very few (perhaps no) perfect associations in social science. Thus, for social factors to be causal, they need only satisfy the four criteria of causality: (a) association (statistical, not deterministic); (b) time order (the cause must precede the consequences); (c) the relationship is not spurious (no third factor, preceding cause and effect in time, is related to both cause and effect); and (d) rationale (the proposed relationship has to make logical sense).

Another problem with the observation that social factors are not related is that they are. Even though abuse can be found among the wealthy and the poor, it is more likely to be found among the poor. Even though most poor people do not abuse their children, wives, or parents, there is indeed a greater risk of abuse among those in the lowest income groups. We will examine the relationship between social factors and family violence in Chapters 3 and 4.

In addition, it is important to point out the dynamic nature of social factors. Changes in social circumstances, such as becoming unemployed or encountering economic problems, can raise the risk of abuse and violence in a family or an intimate relationship.

5. Children who are abused will grow up to be abusers.

This is a myth with some truth value to it. Most studies of wife and child abuse find that abusive adults were more likely to have been treated harshly and abused as children than adults who are not abusive. The problem with the statement that "children who are abused will grow up to be abusers" is that this is a deterministic statement and the relationship is probabilistic. People who experience abuse are more likely, but not preprogrammed, to become violent adults. Sadly, many people have begun to believe that all abused children grow up to be violent. This belief has two negative consequences. First, it scares people who have experienced violence as children into thinking that they are preprogrammed to be violent and that perhaps they should avoid marriage and having children. Second, those who are responsible for detecting and treating child abuse may see an unusual injury in a child and, on learning that a parent had been battered as a child, assume that the parent has caused the injury. False positive diagnoses (labeling someone an abuser when he or she is not) are a possible consequence of believing that violence determines violence.

Again, just as with social factors, it is important to remember that perfect associations rarely exist in social science. Abuse and violence grow out of a complex set of interrelated factors (as we will find in Chapters 3 through 5), and latching onto one commonsense factor misrepresents the causal explanation and can cause injustice.

6. Battered wives "like" being hit and/or are
   responsible for the violence; otherwise, they would leave.

In the wake of the killing of Nicole Brown Simpson and Ronald Goldman, a 911 tape was released by the Los Angeles Police Department. The tape revealed that Nicole Brown Simpson had been beaten by her ex-husband, O.J. During the trial, photographs of the results of one of those beatings were shown to the jury. Although many people reacted to the 911 tape and the photos with sympathy and empathy, others' reactions questioned why she would continue a relationship with a man who had battered her and whom she feared. Many battered women find that when they publicly reveal their victimization, rather than receive sympathy, they are blamed for not leaving their batterers.

One common question asked about battered women is, "Why don't they (the battered wives) just pack up and leave?" Battered women fail to attract the same attention and sympathy directed toward battered children because somehow, many people think that the women (a) provoked the violence and (b) must like it if they didn't leave after the first beating. Those who espouse this view (and it is a belief of both men and women) tend to be those with considerable education, good jobs, and extensive social networks. They cannot imagine that someone could be socially, legally, and materially entrapped in a marriage. They cannot imagine that a woman could literally have no place to go. Wives seem to bear the brunt of considerable "victim blaming." Quite a few people believe that battered wives are somehow culpable, and their culpability is enforced by their decision not to leave. Nothing could be further from the truth. This issue will be discussed at length in Chapter 4.

7. Alcohol and drug abuse are the real causes of violence in the home.

The "demon rum" explanation for abuse in the home is nearly as popular as the mental illness explanation and perhaps more popular than the two social class myths. Again, certain facts help support the myth. Most studies find a considerable association between drinking and violence (Fagan, 1990; Gelles, 1974; Gillen, 1946; Guttmacher, 1960; Snell, Rosenwald, & Robey, 1964; Wolfgang, 1958). In cases of spousal violence, both offender and victim have frequently been drinking before the violence. Perhaps as many as half the instances of violence and abuse involve some alcohol or drugs—a very strong association. But do the drugs or the alcohol themselves cause people to be violent? Are drugs and is alcohol disinhibitors that unleash violent behavior? And would solving the drug or drinking problem eliminate the violence? Common sense frequently says "yes" to these questions. Research argues "no." There is little evidence that alcohol and drugs are disinhibitors. The best evidence against the disinhibitor theory comes from cross-cultural studies of drinking behavior. These studies find that how people react to drinking varies from culture to culture (MacAndrew & Edgerton, 1969). In some cultures, people drink and become violent; in others, people drink and are passive. What explains the difference? The difference is due to what people in those societies believe about alcohol. If they believe it is a disinhibitor, people become disinhibited. If they believe that it is a depressant, people become depressed. Because our society believes that alcohol and drugs release violent tendencies, people are given a "time out" from the normal rules of social behavior when they drink or when people believe they are drunk. Combine the time out with the desire to "hush up" instances of family violence, and you have the perfect excuse: "I didn't know what I was doing, I was drunk." Or from the victim's perspective, "My husband is a Dr. Jekyll and Mr. Hyde—when he drinks he is violent, when he is sober there is no problem." In the end, violent spouses and parents learn that if they want to not be held responsible for their violence, they should either drink before they hit, or at least say they were drunk.

Additional evidence comes from research on the link between alcohol and intimate violence. Murray Straus and his colleagues examined data from two national surveys of family violence. The first survey found that there was a strong relationship between alcohol abuse and family violence. However, extreme levels of alcohol abuse were not related to high levels of violence. Physical violence in families actually declined when drunkenness occurred "almost always" (Coleman & Straus, 1983). Glenda Kaufman Kantor and Murray Straus (1987) examined data from a second survey of family violence and again found that excessive drinking is associated with higher levels of wife abuse. However, in the majority of families, alcohol is not an immediate antecedent of violence.

More recently, drug abuse, especially "crack abuse," has been linked to extreme and severe cases of domestic violence. The issue of the possible link between drug abuse and violence is explosive, and fact is often mixed with myth. One problem is that there are multiple drugs that have been implicated in acts of violence, and each drug has a different physiological effect. In addition, there are varying social expectations for how specific drugs affect human behavior. Research on different forms of drugs and their possible effect on violent behavior has found some consistent evidence. Marijuana produces a euphoric effect and may reduce rather than increase the probability of violent behavior. Research on LSD also finds that the physiological effects of the drug are antithetical with violence. One drug does stand out as a possible cause of violent behavior: amphetamines. Amphetamines raise excitability and muscle tension. This may lead to impulsive behavior. The behavior that follows from amphetamine use is related to both the dosage and preuse personality of the user; high-dosage users who already have aggressive personalities are likely to become more aggressive when using this drug (Johnson, 1972). Studies of nonhuman primates, stump-tailed macaques, have found that the monkeys do become more aggressive when they receive a protocol of d-amphetamine (Smith & Byrd, 1987). Based on his program of research with monkeys and amphetamine, Neil Smith estimates that as much as 5% of instances of physical child abuse are related to amphetamine use and abuse (Smith & Byrd, 1987).

Except for the evidence that appears to link amphetamine use to violence, the picture of the alcohol- and drug-crazed partner or parent who impulsively and violently abuses a family member is a distortion. If alcohol and other drugs are linked to violence at all, it is through a complicated set of individual, situational, and social factors (Gelles, 1993).

8. Violence and love do not coexist in families.

Once people believe that families are violent, they tend to think that the violence occurs all the time. Moreover, the persistent belief is that if family members are violent, they must not love one another. Violence, although common in many families, is certainly not the most frequent behavior in the home. As we will see in Chapters 3, 4, and 5, although violence and abuse are typically chronic problems in families and not simply one-shot events, on average, abusive parents and partners are violent about once every other month. The remaining time the family functions nonviolently (although the threat of physical violence and abuse tends to hang heavy in the air). It is not only possible, but probable, that abused wives still have strong feelings for their husbands. Many battered children love their parents in spite of the beatings. In fact, most victims of family violence are taught that they deserve the beatings, and thus they have the problem, not the attacker. That violence and love can coexist in a household is perhaps the most insidious aspect of family violence, because we grow up learning that it is acceptable to hit the people we love.

What Is Violent and Abusive?

One of the earliest and most enduring problems in the field of child abuse, wife abuse, and family and intimate violence has been to develop useful, clear, and acceptable definitions of *violence* and *abuse*. Those who have studied child abuse have tried for years to develop an acceptable and accepted definition and have found that after countless conferences, workshops, and publications, there are perhaps as many definitions as there are scholars in the field (National Research Council, 1993).

An example of an early definition of child abuse was the one used by C. Henry Kempe and his colleagues (Kempe, Silverman, Steele, & Droegemueller, 1962) in their article "The Battered Child Syndrome." Kempe, a physician, defined child abuse as a clinical condition (i.e., with diagnosable medical and physical symptoms) having to do with those who have been deliberately injured by a physical assault. This definition restricts abuse to only those acts of physical violence that produce a diagnosable injury. The National Center on Child Abuse and Neglect, an agency of the federal government established in 1974, expanded the definition of abuse to include nonphysical acts as well. The agency's definition of abuse is

> the physical or mental injury, sexual abuse, negligent treatment, or mal-treatment of a child under the age of eighteen by a person who is responsible for the child's welfare under circumstances which indicate that the child's health or welfare is harmed or threatened thereby. (Public Law 93-237; 42 U.S.C. 5106g)

This definition lumps acts of omission and commission or acts of violence and nonviolence into the same definition. On the one hand, definitions like those used by the National Center on Child Abuse and Neglect include acts that go well beyond physical violence. On the other hand, this definition is restrictive in that *only* acts of violence that cause an injury are considered abusive.

Force and Violence

If a father takes a gun and shoots at his child and misses, there is no physical injury, and according to many definitions of abuse, this act would not be considered abuse. There is, of course, harm in a father shooting and missing, but the act itself does not qualify as abuse under the strict terms of the definitions. Ideally, then, a definition of abuse should include harmful acts that for some reason (bad aim) do not produce an injury. At the other extreme, a father who spanks his child is not usually considered either abusive or violent. Most people believe that spanking a child is normal, necessary, and good. Nearly 90% of parents report that they spank their children, and some people believe that the true figure is a lot closer to 100%. As many as one in four men and one in six women think that under certain conditions, it is appropriate for a husband to hit his wife (Gelles & Straus, 1988; Stark & McEvoy, 1970). Consequently, some researchers believe that in defining violence, it is a good idea to separate the so-called normal acts of "force" from the nonnormal and harmful acts of "violence." Although such a separation might seem desirable, distinguishing between acceptable and unacceptable acts proves more difficult than one can imagine. One major question is, Who decides which acts of violence are legitimate and illegitimate? Also, is "force" hitting a child without physical evidence of an injury, whereas "violence" is hitting a child and causing a black-and-blue mark? Should the decision be left to the person who is being hit, to the person doing the hitting, to agents of social control such as police, social workers, or judges? Should the decision be left to social scientists? An extensive study of the definitions of child abuse carried out by Jeanne Giovannoni and Rosina Becerra found that what is defined as *child abuse* varies by social category and profession. Police officers, social workers, physicians, and lawyers have differing views on what constitutes child abuse. Similarly, the definition of abuse varies by social class, race, and ethnicity (Giovannoni & Becerra, 1979).

A Definition of Violence

In the end, the difficulty in defining what acts are violent and what acts are physical, but not violent, is due to varying cultural and subcultural views on whether certain behavior is or is not acceptable. It would be far too complex to have a definition that depended on the situation the behavior was used in, the size of the offender, the size of the victim, and the reactions of those who observed or heard about the behavior. For that reason, this book uses the definition of violence employed by a number of researchers. The definition views violence as "an act carried out with the intention or perceived intention of causing physical pain or injury to another person." The physical pain can range from slight pain, as in a slap, to murder. To deal with the commonsense assumption that spankings should be viewed differently from using weapons against wives or children, it is useful to consider two categories of the general definition of violence, "normal" violence and abusive violence.

Normal violence. Normal violence is the commonplace slaps, pushes, shoves, and spankings that frequently are considered a normal or acceptable part of raising children or interacting with a spouse. These are the acts many people object to calling "violent." This is especially true of spanking. Family violence researchers who state their views on television or radio, or who are quoted in the press, often receive indignant letters from people who object to calling a spanking "violent." "Spare the rod and spoil the child." "I was spanked and I needed it." "My little one would be dead by now if I hadn't spanked him and let him know he shouldn't drink or eat certain things." These and other arguments, typically advanced by those who do the hitting, all focus on the physical acts that we consider normal violence.

Abusive violence. The more dangerous acts of violence we shall refer to as abusive violence. These acts are defined as acts that have the high potential for injuring the person being hit. Included in this definition are punches, kicks, bites, chokings, beatings, shootings, stabbings, or attempted shootings or stabbings.

The controversy in this definition is that it does not take into consideration what actually happened to the victims of the violence. By ignoring consequences, this definition is much broader than the more narrow definitions of child or wife abuse, which typically require that some diagnosable harm be inflicted. The reason for not including consequences in the definition is that research on assault and homicide, which has been carried out by criminologists, has consistently found that the things that differentiate injurious violence from violence that causes no harm are typically random phenomena such as aim or luck (Pittman & Handy, 1964; Pokorny, 1965; Wolfgang, 1958).

Why Just Physical Violence?

Hitting, punching, shooting, and other acts of physical violence do not exhaust the range of harmful acts committed by family members against other household members. Students of child maltreatment have identified neglect, emotional abuse, sexual abuse, educational neglect, medical neglect, and failure to thrive as forms of maltreatment. Feminists sometimes argue that pornography and some types of advertising are acts of violence against women (London, 1978).

Physical violence is not the only form of harm that family members and intimate relations experience, nor is it the most harmful form of intimate victimization. Researchers and clinicians have both found that the effect and consequences of emotional or psychological violence are greater and more profound than the consequences of physical victimization alone (Straus & Sweet, 1992; Vissing, Straus, Gelles, & Harrop, 1991). Sexual abuse also has significant harmful consequences (Browne & Finkelhor, 1986). Why, then, does this book focus mainly on physical violence? One reason is pragmatic: Space considerations for this book require me to focus mostly on physical violence in intimate and family relations. Another reason is because it is important, theoretically and practically, to differentiate acts of physical violence from other harmful but nonviolent coercive acts (Etzioni, 1971; Stets, 1990). Physical violence is qualitatively different from other means of injuring people. Thus, although physical violence shares with other harm-producing acts the central characteristics of malevolence and harm-doing intent, the nature of the intended harm—physical pain and suffering—is unique. As the children's taunt goes: "Sticks and stones may break my bones, but names will never hurt me." Well, the names do hurt, and the actual hurt may be more than the physical pain caused by physical violence, but physical and psychological pain are quite different. In addition, lumping all forms of malevolence and harm-doing together may muddy the water so much that it might be impossible to determine what causes abuse. Nevertheless, as space allows, this book will examine the data on extent, correlates, theories, and interventions regarding sexual abuse, emotional and psychological abuse, neglect, and other forms of intimate victimization.

DISCUSSION QUESTIONS

1. Why is it useful to examine all forms of family violence instead of concentrating on just one single type, such as child abuse or violence toward women?

2. Why do the myths and controversies about family violence exist? What possible functions might the myths serve for people who treat family violence? For society?

3. Discuss and critique the "alcohol as a disinhibitor" theory of the relationship between alcohol and family violence.

4. Develop and critique your own definition of *violence* and *abuse*.

5. Discuss whether spanking a child should be considered violence, abuse, or both.

SUGGESTED ASSIGNMENTS

1. Locate newspaper articles that report family violence. What definitions of *violence* and *abuse* seem to be used in these articles? Are any of the myths included in the articles? Identify the common assumptions about the nature and causes of family violence in the articles.

2. Locate articles on child abuse, sexual abuse, or spouse abuse in popular magazines (e.g., *Women's Day, Redbook, Family Circle, Time*, and *Newsweek*). Compare how this issue is presented to the presentation found in newspapers. Locate one or more of the myths or controversies presented in the chapter in the magazine articles.

3. Locate a statistic or fact on some aspect of family and intimate violence presented in a newspaper article or popular magazine. Try to track down the primary source for the statistic or fact. Was the statistic or fact actually accurate? If not, how was the statistic or fact incorrect and what might be the reason for the use of this inaccurate statistic or fact?

4. Interview people about whether they think spanking a child is violent behavior. Examine the social factors related to who defines spankings as violent and who does not (e.g., do definitions vary by sex, age, social position, or some other social factor of the person being interviewed?).

2

VIOLENCE BETWEEN INTIMATES

Historical Legacy—Contemporary Approval

Violence between intimates is not new. The Bible begins with sibling violence—Cain killing Abel (Gen. 4:8). Similarly, there are other biblical descriptions of family violence. Genesis also describes God's commandment that Abraham sacrifice his son Isaac. Later, in the New Testament, Jesus was presumably saved from Herod's "slaughter of the innocents."

If family and intimate violence is not new, perhaps it is more common today than decades or centuries earlier. Many social commentators and some social scientists, noting the apparent increase in reports of family violence and abuse, propose that rising rates of family violence are yet another sign of the disintegration of both the modern family and society in general.

The question of whether we are more violent now than during previous times in history is difficult to answer. The selective inattention to the problem of intimate violence meant that official records of family violence were not kept until the past three decades. Similarly, until the past few decades, researchers were reluctant to conduct surveys and ask questions about violence or abuse. Until the 1980s (see Chapters 3 and 4), there had been no research conducted that attempted to measure the changing rates of violence toward children or between spouses.

The first section of this chapter examines the historical legacy of family violence. Modern Americans are neither the first to use violence on loved ones nor are we the only society in the world to be violent toward those we love. The next section explores the social transformation of violence and traces the evolution of the issue of family violence from selective inattention, when nearly all that was written on violence in the home appeared on the front page of the *National Enquirer*, to the present, when violence between intimates is discussed and analyzed on television and radio talk shows, on television dramas, in national magazines, in legislative bodies, and by presidential task forces. The chapter concludes with a discussion of contemporary attitudes about intimate violence.

The Historical Legacy of
Family and Intimate Violence

We take for granted that today's children have the right to live and grow to achieve their full developmental potential. Women have fought for centuries for equal rights with men. We have begun to take for granted that women have a right to equal treatment. What we take for granted has not always been the case, and the history of the subordination of women and children is closely connected to the history and causes of violence and abuse in the family.

Infanticide and the Abuse of Children

The history of Western society is one in which children have been subjected to unspeakable cruelties. The historian Samuel Radbill (1987) reports that in ancient times, infants had no rights until the right to live was ritually bestowed on them by their fathers. If the right to live was withheld by fathers, infants were abandoned or left to die. Although we do not know how often children were killed or abandoned, we do know that infanticide was widely accepted among ancient and prehistoric cultures. Infants could be put to death because they cried too much, because they were sickly or deformed, or because they had some perceived imperfection. Girls, twins, and the children of unmarried women were the special targets of infanticide (Robin, 1982).

Many societies also subjected their offspring to rituals or survival tests. Some North American Indians threw their newborns into pools of water and rescued them only if they rose to the surface and cried. The Greeks exposed their children to the natural elements as a survival test.

Lloyd DeMause (1974) has examined the history of childhood and graphically explains that by 1526 the latrines of Rome were said to "resound with the cries of children who had been plunged into them" (p. 29). Infanticide continued through the 18th and 19th centuries. Illegitimate children continue to run the greatest risk of infanticide even today. A few years ago, an old steamer trunk was opened in a mill town in southern New Hampshire. Inside the trunk were a number of small skeletons, alleged to have been illegitimate children killed at birth.

Killing children was not the only form of abuse inflicted by generations of parents. From prehistoric times right through colonial America, children were mutilated, beaten, and maltreated. Such treatment was not only condoned, it was often mandated as the most appropriate child-rearing method (Greven, 1990; Miller, 1983; Straus, 1994). Children were hit with rods, canes, and switches. Boys have been castrated to produce eunuchs. Our forefathers in colonial America were implored to "beat the devil" out of their children (Greven, 1990; Straus, 1994). Stubborn-child laws were passed that permitted parents to put to death unruly children, although it is not clear whether children were actually ever killed.

Women: The "Appropriate" Victims

The subordinate status of women in America and in most of the world's societies is well documented. Because physical force and violence are the ultimate resources that can be used to keep subordinate groups in their place, the history of women throughout the world has been one in which women have been victims of physical assault.

The sociologists Rebecca Dobash and Russell Dobash (1979) explain that to understand wife beating in contemporary society, one must understand and recognize the century-old legacy of women as the "appropriate" victims of family violence.

Roman husbands and fathers not only had control over their children but over their wives as well. A Roman husband could chastise, divorce, or kill his wife. Not only that, but the behaviors for which these punishments were appropriate—adultery, public drunkenness, and attending public games—were the very same behaviors that Roman men engaged in daily (Dobash & Dobash, 1979)!

As with children, women's victimization goes as far back as biblical times. Eve is blamed for eating the forbidden fruit. For Eve's transgression, the Bible tells us that all women are to be punished by having to bear children. The very same passage in Genesis that multiplies women's sorrow and calls for them to bear children also sanctions the husband's rule over women (Gen. 3:16).

Although legend has it that Blackstone's codification of English common law in 1768 asserted that a husband had the right to "physically chastise" an errant wife provided that the stick was no thicker than his thumb—and thus the "rule of thumb" was born—such a passage cannot be found in Blackstone (Sommers, 1994). Actually, there have been laws prohibiting wife beating in the United States since the time of the Revolution (Pleck, 1987). However, although the laws existed, they were often indifferently enforced. Furthermore, although the laws outlawed assault and battery and prescribed punishments such as fines and whippings as punishment, courts often allowed a certain amount of chastisement or correction of so-called errant wives "within legal bounds." In 1824, a Mississippi court allowed corporal punishment of wives by husbands. The right to chastise wives was finally overturned by courts in Alabama and Massachusetts in 1871.

Intimate Violence Around the World

Not only does conventional wisdom err when it argues that family violence is a modern phenomenon, it also errs when it asserts that private violence is unique to American families or, if not unique, that the problem is greater in the United States than in other societies.

The anthropologist David Levinson (1981) has examined the records of the Human Relations Area Files at Yale University. These records contain descriptive and statistical information on a wide range of societies over time and around the world. Levinson reports that wife beating is the most common and frequent form of family violence, thus confirming the theory that woman are generally considered the most appropriate victims of intimate violence (see Table 2.1).

Gathering information on family violence in other societies has been difficult. Only the United States, Canada, and Australia have specific

TABLE 2.1   Relationship Between Physical Punishment and
Wife Beating

Wife Beating	Physical Punishment			
	Rare	Infrequent	Frequent	Common
Rare	Andamans Copper Eskimo Ifuago Iroquois Ona Thailand	Rural Irish Hopi Trobrianders		
Infrequent	Kanuri Lapps Lau Mataco Tucano	Klamath Masai Ojibwa Pygmies Santal Taiwan Tikopia Tzeltal	Ashanti Cagaba Garo Pawnee Wolof	
Frequent	Bororo Iban Tarahumara	Kapauku Korea Kurd Toradja	Azande Dogon Somali	Amhara
Common	Chuckchee Tlingit Yanoama	Aymara Hausa	Ganda Truk	Serbs

SOURCE: Levinson (1981); reprinted with permission from *Child Abuse & Neglect, 5*(2), David Levinson, "Physical Punishment of Children and Wifebeating in Cross-Cultural Perspective." Copyright © 1981, Pergamon Press, Ltd.

legislation that requires the reporting of child abuse and neglect; thus, there are no official report data on child or spouse abuse available in other nations. There are, however, an increasing number of local, regional, or national surveys conducted on family violence in other countries.

In 1993, Statistics Canada conducted the first national survey of violence against women in Canada. A telephone survey was conducted with a nationally representative sample of 12,300 women age 18 or older. Of the currently or previously married women, 3 in 10 reported experiencing at least one incident of physical or sexual violence at the hands of a marital partner. Three percent of the women were assaulted by a partner in the year prior to the survey (Rodgers, 1994).

Two national surveys on violence toward women were conducted in New Zealand in 1994. The first study was a survey of a nationally representative sample of 2,000 men, and the second was a follow-up survey of 200 of the 2,000 men. Twenty-one percent of the men surveyed reported committing one act of physical violence against a partner in the previous year, and 53% reported committing an act of emotional abuse. Thirty-five percent of the men reported ever using an act of physical violence, and 62% reported ever using emotional abuse toward a partner (Leibrich, Paulin, & Ransom, 1995).

In addition to these two national surveys, there are other studies that examine the incidence and prevalence of violence against women around the world (United Nations, 1994). The World Bank Discussion Papers, *Violence Against Women: The Hidden Health Burden* (Heise, 1994), describe numerous studies of violence against women. A 1993 study in Chile found that 60% of Chilean women involved in a relationship for 2 or more years had been abused by their male partners (Larrain, 1993). A 1992 study in Ecuador reported that 60% of low-income women had been beaten by a partner. In Japan, 59% of the 769 women surveyed said they were physically abused by a partner (Domestic Violence Research Group, 1993). A Korean study found 38% of Korean women had been battered by a spouse in the past year (Kim & Cho, 1992). Of course, these studies are not really comparable because of varying definitions of violence, abuse, battering, and beating, various survey methodologies, and differing methods of measuring violence. However, collectively the research certainly points out the existence of violence against women in many and varied cultures and societies.

Other research and anecdotal accounts uncover some unique types of violence against women. India, for example, has a problem of dowry-related violence, whereby husbands attack or often burn their wives as a means of extorting more dowry from their wives' families (Prasad, 1994).

There are fewer national surveys of child abuse or child maltreatment. This is because of the great difficulty that occurs when researchers attempt to develop a cross-cultural definition of child maltreatment (Finkelhor & Korbin, 1988; Gelles & Cornell, 1983; Korbin, 1981). Korbin (1981) points out that because there is no universal standard for optimal child rearing, there can be no universal standard for what constitutes child abuse and neglect. Finkelhor and Korbin (1988) explain that a definition of child abuse that could be used internationally should accomplish at least two objectives: (a) It should distinguish child abuse clearly from other social, economic, and health problems of international concern; and (b) it should be sufficiently flexible to apply to a range of situations in a variety of social and cultural contexts. They note that some of what is talked about as child abuse in Western societies has very little meaning in other societies. Finkelhor and Korbin (1988) propose the following definition of child abuse for cross-cultural research: "Child abuse is the portion of harm to children that results from human action that is proscribed (negatively valued), proximate (the action is close to the actual harm— thus, deforesting land that results in child malnutrition does not fit this definition), and preventable (the action could have been avoided)" (p. 4). However, because such a definition has not yet been adopted by re- searchers or put to use in cross-national studies of the extent and patterns of child maltreatment, we have few true cross-cultural studies of child abuse and neglect and must rely on more anecdotal information.

The People's Republic of China has been frequently described as a society with little or no child or wife abuse. However, case examples of severe child abuse in China made their way into the American press in recent years. In the closing months of 1992, three Chinese children were killed by their parents, and their deaths caused an unusual public dis- cussion in China about a problem barely acknowledged in China before ("3 Deaths Trigger Debate," 1992, p. C-3). Although many observers in China viewed these deaths as barbaric, there is the lingering Confucian notion that children must be absolutely obedient to their parents. This, combined with the single-child policy in China and parents' high ambi- tions placed on the one child, has raised concern about possible increases in the problem of physical abuse.

Similarly, Israel is a country where it is thought there is little phys- ical abuse of children. Hanita Zimrin (personal communication, Sep- tember 17, 1991) notes that considerable attention was paid to physical abuse in Israel after a child was beaten to death by a parent on a kibbutz. Zimrin explains, with some irony, that such a case challenged the notion of the "perfect society" and the "perfect child-rearing setting"—the kibbutz.

Scandinavian countries are also described as having few problems with child abuse. This is generally thought to be due to social conditions being good, the widespread use of contraceptives limiting the number of unwanted children, free abortions, and the fact that working mothers can leave their children at day care institutions (Vesterdal, 1977)

My colleague Äke Edfelt and I tested the notion that Scandinavian countries have few problems with child abuse (Gelles & Edfeldt, 1986). Äke Edfeldt, Professor of Education at the University of Stockholm, replicated our national survey of family violence (Straus, Gelles, & Steinmetz, 1980). He translated the Conflict Tactics Scales (Straus, 1979) into Swedish and conducted interviews with a nationally representative sample of 1,168 respondents who had children at home 3 to 17 years of age (this was essentially the same sampling approach we used in our 1976 National Family Violence Survey; Straus et al., 1980).

The results of the comparison between the United States and Sweden were mixed. In general, the Swedish parents reported using less overall violence than did parents in the United States. However, when we confined our analysis to only the most severe and abusive forms of violence, there was no significant difference between the two countries. Whereas differing social conditions may have played a role in limiting spankings, slaps, and other so-called minor acts of violence, parents in both countries are about equally likely to beat, kick, and punch their children.

Students of family violence around the world have tried to synthesize the various data that are available and come up with a general statement that explains why violence toward children is common in some societies and rare in others. The anthropologist Jill Korbin (1981) concludes that if children are valued for economic, spiritual, or psychological qualities, they are less likely to be maltreated. Certain children who are perceived to have undesirable qualities are at greatest risk of abuse. Thus, illegitimate children, orphans, stepchildren, females, or retarded or deformed children are often at greatest risk of abuse. Some students of the new "one child" policy in the People's Republic of China note that an unintended consequence of the law to limit families to one child has been a rather dramatic increase in female infanticide (Korbin, 1981).

Dobash and Dobash (1979) also find that cultural values about women play a role in the risk of wife abuse. The more women are viewed as property of their mates, the greater the risk of abuse.

The Social Transformation of Intimate Violence

The problems of child abuse and wife abuse are not new nor are other forms of family violence—sibling violence and violence toward parents. Perhaps the only new form of family violence is the abuse of elderly persons. This is essentially due to the increase in life expectancy: 50 or 100 years ago, most people simply did not live long enough to become vulnerable to abuse at the hands of their middle-aged children.

Yet although we find cases of family violence throughout recorded history, viewing family violence as a social issue and a social problem is a relatively new phenomenon. For most of the time there has been violence between loved ones, it has literally and figuratively occurred behind closed doors. It gradually became both a social issue, that is, a condition that captures public attention and generates concern, controversy, and in some cases collective action, and a social problem, that is, a condition found to be harmful to individual and societal well-being.

It is tempting to look for some dramatic change that took place 30 years ago that propelled family violence out from behind closed doors into the public spotlight. That, however, would be naive. Rather, violence in the home came to public attention gradually. The fortress doors of the private family did not swing open, they moved inch by inch over the decades.

Discovering Childhood and Children

The historical treatment of children is not entirely bleak. Children's rights were recognized, but slowly. Six thousand years ago, children in Mesopotamia had a patron goddess to look after them. The Greeks and Romans had orphan homes. Some historical accounts also mention the existence of foster care for children. Samuel Radbill (1987) reports that child protection laws were legislated as long ago as 450 B.C. At the same time, the father's complete control over his children was modified. Anthropologists have noted that nearly every society has laws and rules regarding sexual access to children.

The social historian Phillipe Aries, in his book *Centuries of Childhood* (1962), claims that the concept of childhood as a distinct stage emerged after the Middle Ages (from about 400 A.D. to 1000 A.D.). Before then, childhood as a stage ended when an infant was weaned. Children were seen as miniature adults and were portrayed as such in the artwork of the

Middle Ages. Paintings and sculptures of children pictured them with little heads and miniature adult bodies, dressed in adult clothing. Renaissance art was the first time children were portrayed as children.

Michael Robin (1982) has traced the roots of child protection. He found that the Renaissance, a 300-year period spanning 1300 to 1600, was the beginning of a new morality regarding children. Children were seen as a dependent class in need of the protection of society. This was also a time when the family was looked to for teaching children the proper rules of behavior. At the same time, the power of the father increased dramatically.

Although society paid more attention to children, this was not without some dire consequences. Puritan parents in colonial America were instructed by leaders such as Cotton Mather that strict discipline of children could not begin too early (Greven, 1990).

The Enlightenment of the 18th century brought children increased attention and services. The London Foundling Hospital was founded during this period. The hospital not only provided pediatric care but, as Robin (1982) recounts, was also the center of the moral reform movement on behalf of children.

In the United States, the case of Mary Ellen Wilson is almost always singled out as the turning point in concern for children's welfare. In 1874, 8-year-old Mary Ellen lived in the home of Francis and Mary Connolly but was not the blood relative of either. Mary Ellen was the illegitimate daughter of Mary Connolly's first husband. A neighbor noticed the plight of Mary Ellen, who was beaten with a leather thong and allowed to go ill clothed in bad weather. The neighbor reported the case to Etta Wheeler, a "friendly visitor" who worked for St. Luke's Methodist Mission. In the mid-1800s, child welfare was church based rather than government based. Wheeler turned to the police and the New York City Department of Charities for help for Mary Ellen Wilson and was turned down—first by the police, who said there was no proof of a crime, and second by the charity agency, who said they did not have custody of Mary Ellen. The legend goes on to note that Henry Berge, founder of the Society for the Prevention of Cruelty to Animals, intervened on behalf of Mary Ellen, and the courts accepted the case because Mary Ellen was a member of the animal kingdom. In reality, the court reviewed the case because the child needed protection. The case was argued not by Henry Berge, but by his colleague, Elbridge Gerry.

Mary Ellen Wilson was removed from her foster home and initially placed in an orphanage. Her foster mother was imprisoned for a year, and the case received detailed press coverage for months. In December 1874, the New York Society for the Prevention of Cruelty to Children was founded.

Protective societies rose and fell during the next 80 years. The political scientist Barbara Nelson (1984) notes that by the 1950s public interest in abuse and neglect was practically nonexistent. Technology helped to pave the way for the rediscovery of child abuse. In 1946, the radiologist John Caffey (1946) reported on a number of cases of children who had multiple long-bone fractures and subdural hematomas. Caffey used X rays to identify the fractures, although he did not speculate about the causes. In 1953, P. V. Woolley and W. A. Evans (1955) did speculate that the injuries might have been inflicted by the children's parents. Caffey (1957) looked again at his X-ray data and speculated that such injuries could have been inflicted by parents or caretakers. By 1962, the physician C. Henry Kempe and his colleagues at the University of Colorado Medical Center (Kempe et al., 1962) were quite certain that many of the injuries they were seeing and the healed fractures that appeared on X rays were intentionally inflicted by parents.

Kempe's article became the benchmark of the public and professional rediscovery of child abuse. Kempe's article and a strong editorial that accompanied the article created considerable public and professional concern. *Time, Newsweek,* the *Saturday Evening Post,* and *Life* followed up the Kempe article with news or feature stories. Barbara Nelson (1984) has traced the record of professional and mass media articles on child abuse and neglect. Prior to 1962, it was unusual that a single mass media article on abuse would be published in a year. After Kempe's article, there was a tenfold increase in popular articles that discussed child abuse. Today, a year does not go by without each major periodical publishing at least one cover story on child abuse. Kempe founded his own professional journal, *Child Abuse & Neglect: The International Journal,* and thousands of professional articles are published annually in medical, sociology, psychology, social work, and other scholarly journals. There are now nearly a dozen scientific journals devoted to family and intimate violence in general, or some aspect of family violence such as sexual or emotional abuse.

That public and professional media coverage of child abuse grew rapidly and in tandem was not a coincidence. Each professional journal article produced additional fodder for the mass media (many scholars and scholarly journals issue press releases to accompany publication of a new article). Each popular article added legitimacy to the public concern for abuse and stimulated a new round of research and scholarly publication.

The symbiotic relationship between scholarly and popular media was not without some problems. The translation of scientific writing into popular presentation often leveled, sharpened, or distorted the scientific findings and statements. For instance, the editorial that accompanied Kempe's article in the *Journal of the American Medical Association* said that "it is likely that [the battered child syndrome] will be found to be a more frequent cause of death than such well recognized and thoroughly studied diseases as leukemia, cystic fibrosis and muscular dystrophy and might rank well above automobile accidents" ("The Battered-Child Syndrome," 1962, p. 42). By the time the statement in the editorial had found its way to the public press, it had been slightly changed to state that child abuse was one of the five leading causes of death of children, even though at the time there were no actual data to support such an assertion. Similarly, estimates of the incidence of child abuse and the possible causes were stated and restated so often that they took on lives of their own apart from the initial speculative presentations in scholarly journals.

Two other forces worked to move child abuse out from behind closed doors during the 1960s. The first was the passage of child abuse reporting laws, and the second was the effort in the federal government to focus concern on the plight of abused children.

One of the concrete consequences of the rediscovery of child abuse after the publication of Kempe's 1962 article on the battered child syndrome was the passage of child abuse reporting laws in each of the 50 states between 1963 and 1967. Reporting laws were the quickest, most concrete measure states could take to demonstrate that they wanted to "do something" about the abuse of children. The underlying theme of many of the popular and professional publications on child abuse from the time of Mary Ellen Wilson was the fact that abused children were "missing persons" in social and criminal justice agencies. Many abused children came to public attention only at the point of death. Logic seemed to dictate that if society were to help abused children, it would have to identify those in need of help. Not coincidentally, child abuse reporting laws were often viewed as a no- or low-cost means for state legislators to do something about abuse. Few legislators who jumped on the reporting law bandwagon could foresee that reporting laws would lead to uncovering millions of children who required state-funded protective services. The myth that family violence was rare had such a strong hold that most legislators assumed that the laws they passed would lead to uncovering only a handful of abused and neglected children in their state.

The Children's Bureau, first an agency in the Department of Labor, then an agency of the Department of Health, Education, and Welfare, and finally located within the Department of Health and Human Services, was the first federal focal point of discussion and concern for abused children. The Children's Bureau was active in the cause of abused children as far back as the 1950s. The bureau was founded in 1912 by an act of Congress with the mandate of disseminating information on child development. The bureau also acquired the budget and mandate to conduct research on issues concerning child development. The Children's Bureau engaged in a variety of activities regarding child abuse and neglect. The agency participated in one of the earliest national meetings on child abuse sponsored by the Children's Division of the American Humane Association. After the publication of Kempe's 1962 article, the bureau convened a meeting to draft a model child abuse reporting law. The model law was drafted in 1963. Finally, the bureau funded a variety of research projects, including David Gil's first national survey of officially reported cases of child abuse. In 1974, Congress enacted the Child Abuse Prevention and Treatment Act and located the National Center on Child Abuse and Neglect in the Children's Bureau.

Congressional interest in child abuse prior to 1973 was limited to the passage of a reporting law for the District of Columbia and some attempts to pass national reporting laws. In 1973, then Senator Walter Mondale introduced the Child Abuse Prevention and Treatment Act (42 U.S.C. 5101). The act, enacted in 1974, defined child abuse and neglect, established the National Center on Child Abuse and Neglect, set forth a budget for research and demonstration projects, and called for a national survey of the incidence of child abuse and neglect.

Child abuse appeared to be a "safe" congressional issue. Again, the myth that abuse was rare and confined to the mentally disturbed seemed to limit the scope of the problem and the need for large, federal spending. Who could disagree, after seeing slides of horribly abused children, that such children did not need care and protection? Mondale needed a safe issue. He had seen his Comprehensive Child Development Act vetoed by then President Nixon. Even Nixon, Mondale would say, could not be in favor of child abuse.

Child abuse was not as safe an issue as it first seemed. Although one witness at Mondale's Senate hearings on the Child Abuse Prevention and Treatment Act, Jolly K., a former child abuser and founder of Parents Anonymous, captured media and congressional attention with her testimony recounting her abuse of her child, another witness, the social welfare expert David Gil, showed the "unsafe" side of the issue when he insisted on linking abuse to poverty. Moreover, Gil went beyond the narrow scope of the public stereotype of child abuse and introduced the issue of corporal punishment and spanking into his testimony. Finally, Gil concluded that the bill as written was too narrow to identify, treat, and prevent the real problem.

The Child Abuse Prevention and Treatment Act passed. It was never clear whether President Nixon could be against child abuse—he signed the bill in the midst of mounting public clamor over Watergate. The final amount of money made available for research and demonstration projects was relatively small, $85 million. Many child abuse experts who realized how extensive the problem was and how difficult it would be to treat suggested that such a trifling amount was but a rounding error at the Pentagon. Yet despite concern over the scope of the legislation and the narrowness of the mandate of the law, the passage of the Child Abuse Prevention and Treatment Act succeeded in creating a federal presence and a federal bureaucracy that could serve as a focal point of public and professional awareness of child abuse and neglect.

Discovering Wife Abuse

There was no Mary Ellen for battered women, no technological breakthroughs such as pediatric radiology to uncover years of broken jaws and broken bones. No medical champion would capture public and professional attention in the way Kempe had for battered children. There was no "Women's Bureau" in the federal government. And initially, there was no powerful senator who used a congressional committee chairmanship as a bully pulpit to bring attention to the plight of battered women.

The discovery of wife abuse was a traditional grassroots effort. Attention to the problem of wife battering came from women themselves. A women's center in the Chiswick section of London founded by Erin Pizzey became a refuge for victims of battering. Pizzey wrote the first book on wife abuse, *Scream Quietly or the Neighbors Will Hear* (1974), and produced a documentary movie of the same name. Both captured the attention of women in Europe and the United States. Women's groups began to organize safe houses or battered wife shelters as early as 1972 in the United States. The National Organization for Women created a task force to examine wife battering in 1975.

The results of research on wife abuse in the United States began to be published in 1973. The data on the extent of the problem, the patterns of violence, factors associated with wife abuse, and other analyses were quickly seized on by those who believed that the abuse of women deserved the same place on the public agenda that child abuse had attained. As with child abuse, the scholarly publications fed media articles and the media articles fed public interest, which led to more research and professional attention.

Still, by the early 1980s, public and professional interest in wife battering had lagged far behind interest in child abuse. There were some congressional hearings on wife abuse and then Congresswoman Barbara Milkulski introduced legislation for a National Domestic Violence Prevention and Treatment Act. A federal Office of Domestic Violence was established in 1979 only to be closed in 1981.

Some progress was made in the mid-1980s. The National Domestic Violence Prevention and Treatment Act (42 U.S.C. 13701) was passed into law, although spending from this legislation was but a trickle. The U.S. Attorney General's Task Force on Family Violence held hearings across the country in 1984 and published the final report in September 1984.

The year 1994 was a watershed year for the issue of violence against women. Perhaps not coincidentally, this was the year that Nicole Brown Simpson and Ron Goldman were murdered and Brown Simpson's ex-husband, O.J. Simpson, was charged with the murder. At about the same time the murders took place, Congress was completing the 1994

Violent Crime Control and Law Enforcement Act, which included Title IV, the Violence Against Women Act (VAWA). This crime bill, with the VAWA, was passed by Congress in August 1994 and was signed into law by President Clinton on September 13, 1994. The VAWA appropriated $1.5 billion to fight violence against women, including $3 million over 3 years to reestablish a national hot line to help victims and survivors of domestic violence. An additional $26 million was appropriated for state grants that would encourage states to take more creative, innovative, and effective approaches in law enforcement and prosecutor training; development and expansion of law enforcement and prosecution, such as special domestic violence units; improved data collection and communication strategies; improved victim service programs; and improved programs concerning stalking. The VAWA also included various provisions to increase protection of battered women, including a civil rights title that declared "all persons in the United States shall have the right to be free from crimes of violence motivated by gender." Last, an office on domestic violence was established within the U.S. Department of Justice.

At about the same time the VAWA was passed, the Family Violence Prevention Fund, along with the Advertising Council, began a national public awareness campaign titled "No Excuse for Domestic Violence." Public service announcements that were designed to educate the public about domestic violence and promote prevention and intervention appeared on television and in newspapers.

Legal reforms also occurred at the state level. States enacted legislation designed to establish domestic violence prosecution units, to criminalize sexual assault of wives by their husbands or ex-husbands, to improve protection for victims of stalking, and to develop more effective legal sanctions for domestic violence offenders.

A Concern for Private Violence

It is tempting to give credit for the discovery of a social problem to a single great person or a single tragic event. The field of child abuse and neglect certainly owes much to the late C. Henry Kempe. Walter Mondale was thought a hero by those concerned for child protection, and Senator Joseph Biden was instrumental in passing the Violence Against Women Act.

Another point of view is that no single person, journal article, or piece of legislation propels a problem from obscurity onto the public agenda. Rather, an issue slowly and gradually becomes a public issue.

The "great man" and the slow social movement explanations of the social transformation of family violence are inadequate. Rather, a variety of social movements and social concerns combined in the late 1960s to create a climate where people were ready and willing to listen to those concerned with the victimization of women and children.

The assassinations of John F. Kennedy, Robert Kennedy, and Martin Luther King, Jr. focused public concern on violence. The focus led to the establishment of the President's Commission on the Causes and Prevention of Violence. The commission's national survey on attitudes and experience with violence produced invaluable data for researchers in the field of family violence.

The 1960s were also a period of violent social protest and race riots, again focusing public concern on violence. The baby boomers of the 1950s were teenagers in the 1960s, and as is the case for those 18 to 24 years of age, they engaged in innumerable acts of delinquency and violence, pushing up the national homicide, assault, and rape rates. The public believed that we were in the midst of an epidemic of violence. Fear of violent crime began to paralyze American society. The Figgie Report, published in 1980, found that 4 out of 10 Americans were afraid of being assaulted, robbed, raped, or murdered in their homes or on the streets where they lived and worked.

Concern for violence would not have meant much had it not occurred at the same time as we were undergoing a resurgence of both the women's and the children's movements. These existing social movements provided the forum, the workers, and the energy to collect, organize, and present information on private victimization. Existing national groups who lobbied on behalf of women and children made it easier to lobby for national and regional attention to the problems of the abuse of women and children.

A final necessary and sufficient piece that made the puzzle into a portrait of a problem was the research being carried out by social and behavioral scientists. Until there could be scientific data that shattered the myths of abuse, it was impossible to convince the public and legislators that family violence was a legitimate problem deserving a continued place on the national agenda.

Contemporary Attitudes

Violence between family members has a historical tradition that goes back centuries and cuts across continents. It should come as no surprise that contemporary social scientists have proposed that in the United States and many other countries, "the marriage license is a hitting license" (Straus et al., 1980). Numerous surveys and situations emphasize the point that today in the United States some people still believe that under certain circumstances, it is perfectly appropriate for a husband to hit his wife. The parents who fail to hit their children are considered to be deviant, not the parents who hit.

At the end of the 1960s, the U.S. Commission on the Causes and Prevention of Violence carried out a study of violence in the United States. The primary purpose of the study was to try to understand the causes of the tragic rash of assassinations and riots that plagued the country between 1963 and 1968. Along with the questions on public violence, the commission asked a number of questions about private violence. Among the conclusions was that about one quarter of all adult men, and one in six adult women, said they could think of circumstances in which it would be all right for a husband to hit his wife or for the wife to hit her husband. Overall, about one in five (21%) of those surveyed approved of a husband slapping his wife (Stark & McEvoy, 1970). The same survey found that 86% of those surveyed agreed that young people needed "strong" discipline. Of the sample, 70% thought that it was important for a boy to have a few fist fights while he was growing up.

Fifteen years after the U.S. Commission on the Causes and Prevention of Violence conducted their research, my colleagues Murray Straus and Suzanne Steinmetz and I carried out the first national survey on family violence. Our questions of people's attitudes toward violence in the home confirmed the findings from earlier research. Just under one in four wives and one in three husbands thought that a couple slapping one another was at least somewhat necessary, normal, and good (Straus et al., 1980, p. 47). More than 70% of those questioned thought that slapping a 12-year-old child was either necessary, normal, or good.

Anecdotal accounts further underscore the widespread cultural approval of private violence. In 1964, a young woman named Kitty Genovese was returning home to her apartment in the Queens section of New York City. She was accosted and repeatedly stabbed by a man, and although a number of her neighbors heard her screams for help and watched the assault from windows, no one called the police. The young woman's death led many people to conclude that American society was corrupt, because bystanders seemed too apathetic or unwilling to get involved in a homicide. However, on closer examination, it was suggested that the apathy of Kitty Genovese's neighbors was not the result of their lack of concern, or the fact that they were immune to violence after years of watching television. Rather, many of the witnesses thought that they were seeing a man beating his wife, and that, after all, is a family matter.

In Worcester, Massachusetts, a district court judge sat on the bench and tried an occasional wife abuse case despite the fact that he was a wife beater who misrepresented his behavior under oath during a divorce trial (D'Agostino, 1983).

Millions laughed (and still laugh) when Jackie Gleason would rant, "Alice, [you're going] to the moon" while shaking an angry fist at his television wife in the popular program "The Honeymooners."

Fairy tales, folklore, and nursery rhymes are full of violence against children. Hansel and Gretel, before they were lured into the gingerbread house, had been abandoned by their parents to starve in the forest because money was scarce. Snow White was taken in the woods to be killed by the huntsman on the order of the wicked queen, who was her stepmother. Mother Goose's "Old Woman Who Lived in a Shoe" beat her children soundly and sent them to bed. "Humpty Dumpty" is a thinly disguised metaphor for the fragility of children, and "Rock-a-Bye Baby," with the cradle falling from the tree, is not even thinly disguised.

Changing Attitudes

There is evidence from surveys that attitudes regarding family violence are changing. Murray Straus and I repeated our National Family Violence Survey in 1985. Approval for a husband slapping his wife and a wife slapping her husband declined from 1975. In 1985, only 13% of those surveyed could approve of a husband slapping his wife in some situations. The level of approval of a husband slapping his wife declined to 12% in

1992 and further declined to 10% in 1994. Approval for a wife slapping her husband stayed relatively unchanged between 1968 and 1994 with about one in five respondents approving of a wife slapping her husband in some situations (Gelles & Straus, 1988; Straus, Kaufman Kantor, & Moore, 1994).

Other surveys also find decreasing public tolerance for violence against women. Surveys conducted for the Family Violence Prevention Fund found that four in five surveyed consider domestic violence an extremely important social issue, ranking it more important than teen alcoholism and pregnancy and about as important as the environment. An increasing number of Americans believe outside intervention is needed if a man hits his wife (87% agreed in 1995 compared with 80% in 1994). In the 1995 survey, 57% of men agreed that abusers should be arrested compared with 49% agreement in 1994 (Family Violence Prevention Fund, 1995).

The trend of contemporary attitudes regarding violence against children is more mixed. There has been a steady increase in the proportion of the public who disapprove of child abuse and neglect. The National Committee to Prevent Child Abuse has conducted annual public opinion polls since 1987 to measure the extent to which the public perceives child abuse to be a serious social problem, as well as the extent to which the public is committed to preventing the abuse of children. Each survey found that the majority of the public viewed physical punishment and repeated yelling and swearing as harmful to children's well-being. In 1995, only 22% of the public felt that physical punishment *never* leads to injury and only 6% believed repeated yelling and swearing *never* leads to long-term emotional harm (Daro, 1995; Daro & Gelles, 1992).

Paradoxically, although the general public appears more willing to view physical punishment and yelling and swearing as harmful, the public still endorses spanking. The National Opinion Research Center's General Social Survey found that in 1991, 73% of adults agree that it is sometimes necessary to discipline a child with a good hard spanking. This is down from 83% for the period 1983-1987 (National Opinion Research Center, 1991).

Summary

The chapters that follow (a) document the extent of intimate violence in the United States today, (b) consider the factors that are associated with acts of intimate violence, (c) examine the various theories that have been brought to bear to explain violence in the home, and (d) consider methods of treating and preventing family violence. The tragic nature of family violence and the emotions that are stirred up as a result of specific instances of child, wife, or elder abuse frequently focus our attention on the immediate situation or on a specific case. It is important to keep in mind that what we are experiencing is neither new nor particularly unique to our own society. While we look for causes and solutions in individuals, in families, or even in communities, we should remember that cultural attitudes about women, children, and elders and cultural attitudes about violence as a means of self-expression and solving problems are at the root of private violence. We will see that income, stress, and other social-psychological factors are related to acts and patterns of intimate violence, but we also need to consider that people have choices as to how they will respond to stress, crisis, and unhappiness. The historical and cultural legacy of violence in the home is a powerful means of influencing what choices people consider appropriate. Sociologists David Owens and Murray Straus (1975) found that experience with violence as a child is one of the most powerful contributors to attitudes that approve of interpersonal violence. We now turn to an examination of violence toward children.

DISCUSSION QUESTIONS

1. Why are women considered the "appropriate" victims of family violence?

2. Identify the problems that hamper our ability to compare the extent of family violence in other Western and non-Western societies to the extent of family violence in the United States.

3. What factors explain why violence toward children is common in some societies and rare in others?

SUGGESTED ASSIGNMENTS

1. Read some of the Old and New Testaments of the Bible and identify examples of family violence (implicit or explicit).

2. Read some Mother Goose nursery rhymes and identify themes or messages that seem to condone violence and abuse of children. Find other children's stories or fables that convey the same message.

3. Watch Saturday morning cartoon shows and count how many violent acts are included per 10-minute segment.

3

Violence Toward Children

Sue was a single parent who lived in a fourth-floor walk-up apartment. Her husband had left her 3 years earlier, and child support payments stopped within weeks of the final divorce decree. Poverty and illness were as much a part of Sue's home as the busy activity of her 4-year-old daughter, Nancy. One cold, gray March afternoon, Sue took Nancy out for a walk. Together they hiked up the steep pedestrian walkway of a suspension bridge that rose up behind their apartment. At the top of the bridge, Sue hugged Nancy and then threw her off the bridge. Sue jumped a moment later.

Miraculously, both Nancy and Sue survived. Both were plucked from the icy water by a fishing boat. Nancy, with major internal injuries, was rushed to a nearby hospital, and Sue, remarkably without major injury, was sped to a different hospital. Nancy joined the thousands of children each year who are admitted to hospitals for child abuse. Her case, and that of her mother, was starkly clear. It involved an intentional act designed to grossly injure, harm, or kill a child. The child abuse team at the hospital that admitted Nancy had little trouble diagnosing Nancy's condition and immediately filed both a child abuse report and a restraining order that

41

would keep Sue from removing Nancy from the hospital. When, after 6 months, Nancy was ready to be released, the hospital's attorneys filed a petition to terminate Sue's parental rights. The attorneys argued that Nancy would be best placed in a foster home or institution, rather than being given to a relative (they suspected that there was considerable violence in the homes of Nancy's grandparents and aunts and uncles).

Few would question that Nancy was an abused child. Few would question the wisdom of the hospital in taking steps to assure that Nancy would be protected from further violence and injury. The case of Sue and Nancy (not their real names, and a composite of a number of child abuse cases), is unusual. It is unusual because the intent of the parent and the cause of the injury were so obvious. In the normal case, a hospital child abuse diagnostic team, or a team of social workers, does not have clear evidence about how an injury to a child occurred. More common is the case of a child who is observed at school or in a hospital emergency room with a cut, a bruise, or some other injury. Physical examinations, interviews with the child and the parent, and an examination of the child's medical history (if available) can sometimes help unravel the case and separate true accidents from inflicted injuries. When a child experiences violence that does not produce a black-and-blue mark, cut, or injury, determining whether the child has been harmed is even more complex, because variable community standards and definitions of abuse have to be applied to an act that has produced no gross visible harm. Diagnosing emotional abuse, psychological abuse, and sexual abuse are even more difficult, because these forms of maltreatment rarely leave overt physical signs of injury.

Determining the extent of child abuse and violence toward children in the United States is a difficult task because not all cases of abuse and violence are as obvious as Nancy and Sue's. Estimates of the extent of abuse vary, as do definitions and community standards. This chapter begins by reviewing various sources of information on the extent and nature of violence, abuse, and the maltreatment of children. Before considering who abuses children, we consider the process by which child abuse is recognized and reported in the United States. Official reports of child abuse tend to overrepresent some populations—poor and minority families—and underrepresent other families—middle class and professionals—in part because minority and poor families are more likely to be identified and reported for maltreatment. As a result, relying on these reports as a basis for estimating extent and patterns of child maltreatment leads to the perpetuation of some of the myths I discussed in Chapter 1 (e.g., only poor people abuse their children). Finally, the chapter reviews the evidence on the consequences of child abuse.

The Extent of Violence and Maltreatment

Physical Punishment

Spanking children is perhaps the most common form of family violence in the United States, and because it is considered acceptable and appropriate, many people object to calling it a case of family violence. Nevertheless, the main objective of a spanking or slapping of a child is to teach the child a lesson, to get the child to stop a certain behavior (running into the street, touching a hot stove), or to relieve a parent's own pent-up frustration. As we saw in the previous chapter, many parents feel that children *need* to be hit. Justifications from a number of parents illustrate this attitude:

> I spank her once a week—when she deserves it—usually when she is eating. I believe that a child should eat so much and that is it.
>
> Once in a great while I use a strap. I don't believe in hitting in the head or in the face—although, Rhoda, I slapped her in her face a couple of times because she was sassing. *That* she needed.
>
> But right now she doesn't understand that much. I mean you can't stand and explain really something in detail that she'll understand. So I slap sometimes. She understands when she gets a slap when she's done something wrong. (Gelles, 1974, pp. 62-63)

Of course, if the slight spanking or slap does not work, the parent will typically hit a little harder, at least until the child "gets the message."

> I used to use my hand—put them over my knee and give them a good swat. But then I got myself a little paddle—the ball broke off and I kept the paddle. (Gelles, 1974, p. 69)

Because the intent is to cause some slight harm so that the child will get the message, physical punishment, whether in the best interests of the child or not, is consistent with our definition of violence as described in Chapter 1.

Social surveys indicate that physical punishment of children is used by 84% to 97% of all parents at some time in their children's lives (Blumberg, 1964; Bronfenbrenner, 1958; Erlanger, 1974; Stark & McEvoy, 1970; Straus, 1994; Straus & Gelles, 1990). Despite parents' descriptions of how and why they use violence, and the claim that physical punishment is used because parents cannot reason with very young children, physical punishment of children does not cease when the children are old enough to walk, talk, or reason with (Wauchope & Straus, 1990). Four studies of college and university students found that half were hit when they were seniors in high school (Mulligan, 1977; Steinmetz, 1971; Straus, 1971; Wolfner, 1996). One of these studies (Mulligan, 1977) reported that 8% of the students questioned reported that they had been "physically injured" by their parents during the last year they lived at home before entering college.[1]

Child Abuse and Neglect

Various techniques have been used in attempts to achieve an accurate estimate of child abuse in the United States. In 1967, David Gil (1970) conducted a nationwide inventory of reported cases of physical child abuse (before, however, all 50 states had enacted mandatory reporting laws). He found 6,000 confirmed cases of child abuse. Gil also reported on an opinion survey that asked a representative sample of 1,520 adults if they had personal knowledge of families where incidents of child abuse had occurred. Forty-five, or 3% of the sample, reported knowledge of 48 different incidents. Extrapolating this number to a national population of 110 million adults, Gil estimated that between 2.53 and 4.07 million children were abused each year, or between 13.3 and 21.4 incidents of abuse per 1,000 persons in the United States. Gil's data were later analyzed by Richard Light (1974) to correct for possible instances where the same abusive incidents were known by more than one person (Light assumed that if one adult in a household knew about the incident, then other household members might also know). Light's refined estimate was that there were 500,000 abused children in the United States during the year Gil conducted his survey.

Other investigators in the 1970s tried to estimate how many children were physically abused by their parents. Saad Nagi (1975) surveyed community agencies that had contact with abused children. He estimated that 167,000 cases of abuse were reported annually in the mid-1970s, and an additional 91,000 cases went unreported. Nagi estimated that there were 950,000 reportable cases of abuse and neglect each year—two thirds of which were reported, and one third of which were not. Vincent DeFrancis, then with the American Humane Association, testified before the U.S. Senate in 1973 and estimated that there were 30,000 to 40,000 truly abused children in the United States. Physician Vincent Fontana (1973) placed the figures as high as 1.5 million.

Studies of reported child maltreatment. As is evident, in the 1970s there were guesstimates of the extent of child abuse for every guesser. In the 1980s, researchers and the federal government refined their methods of measuring the extent of child maltreatment. Current research on reported and recognized child maltreatment sheds some scientific light on how common abuse is. Although the studies are different in method, purpose, and findings, they do agree that abuse is considerably more common than people in the 1960s and even 1970s believed.

The National Center on Child Abuse and Neglect has conducted three surveys designed to measure the national incidence of reported and recognized child maltreatment (Burgdorf, 1980; National Center on Child Abuse and Neglect, 1988, 1996). All three assessed how many cases were known to investigatory agencies and how many cases were known to professionals in schools, hospitals, and other social service agencies.

Table 3.1 presents a summary of the preliminary incidence estimates of the six major types of child maltreatment as well as data on the severity of the impairment caused by the maltreatment. For the most recent survey, a total of 2.9 million maltreated children were known by the agencies surveyed in the study in 1993. Of the total number of maltreated children, an estimated 630,800 (9.2 per 1,000) were physically abused; 302,000 children (4.4 per 1,000) were sexually abused; 536,400 children (7.9 per 1,000) were emotionally abused, and 2,481,800 children (36.4 per 1,000) were neglected (physical neglect, emotional neglect, and educational neglect).

TABLE 3.1   Estimates of Total Number of Maltreated Children, 1993

Maltreatment Type	Total Number of Cases
Physical abuse	630,800
Sexual abuse	302,000
Emotional abuse	536,400
Neglect	2,481,800
Physical	1,368,200
Emotional	583,600
Educational	530,000
Seriously injured children	572,200

SOURCE: Based on data from "Preliminary Findings Regarding Child Abuse and Neglect" (1995, September 18). National Center on Child Abuse and Neglect.

A second source of data on the extent of child maltreatment comes from the National Child Abuse and Neglect Data System (NCANDS). NCANDS is a national data collection and analysis project carried out by the National Center on Child Abuse and Neglect (U.S. Department of Health and Human Services, National Center on Child Abuse and Neglect, 1996).[2] The data are official report data collected from all 50 states and the District of Columbia.

In 1994, states received 2.9 million reports of child maltreatment, representing 2,935,470 individual child victims. Of the 1,197,133 child victims for whom maltreatment was indicated or substantiated and for whom there were data on type of maltreatment,[3] 258,320 experienced physical abuse (3.8 per 1,000); 535,510 experienced neglect other than medical neglect (7.9 per 1,000); 25,018 experienced medical neglect (less than 0.1 per 1,000); 139,980 experienced sexual abuse (2 per 1,000); 47,610 experienced emotional maltreatment (less than 0.1 per 1,000); 149,235 children were classified as experiencing other forms of maltreatment (2 per 1,000); and 41,460 experienced unknown forms of maltreatment.

The National Committee to Prevent Child Abuse also collects data from states on child abuse and neglect reporting (Weise & Daro, 1995). The 1995 survey found that there were an estimated 3,140,000 children reported for child maltreatment in 1994. Of these, 33% were substantiated, for an estimate of 1,036,000 maltreated children in 1994, or a rate of 16 per 1,000 children.[4] Twenty-one percent of the substantiated cases, or 217,560 children, were physically abused; 49%, or 507,640 children, were neglected; 11%, or 113,960, were sexually abused; 3%, or 31,080, were emotionally abused; and the remaining 16%, 165,760, were classified as "other" maltreatment.

There are problems with all the estimates of the extent of child maltreatment that are based on official reports. First, definitions of maltreatment—including physical abuse—and reporting practices vary from state to state and from agency to agency. Each profession has a somewhat different definition of child abuse. Second, individual, agency, and state participation in the surveys is variable. Some states provide complete data to the National Center on Child Abuse and Neglect; other states do not provide complete data. The national survey of cases that were known by professionals also had problems, with some agencies fully cooperating and others failing to take part or providing only the most meager help.

National self-report surveys of family violence. A source of data *not based* on official reports or official awareness, but limited to only one aspect of child maltreatment—physical violence—are the surveys carried out in 1976 and again in 1985 by Murray Straus and Richard Gelles (Gelles & Straus, 1987, 1988; Straus & Gelles, 1986, 1990; Straus, Gelles, & Steinmetz, 1980). Straus and Gelles conducted two studies on the subject of family violence, using nationally representative samples of 2,146 individual family members in 1976 and 6,002 family members in 1985. One part of the study focused on the homes where children under the age of 18 lived. Parents in these homes were asked to report on their own "conflict tactics techniques" with their children. Among the list of conflict tactics were nine items that dealt with physical violence. These items ranged from pushing and shoving to the use of a knife or gun (see Table 3.2 for a list of the violence items). The milder forms of violence were, of course, the most common. However, even with the severe forms of violence, the rates were surprisingly high:

- Of the parents surveyed, 1.5% reported that they kick, bite, or punch their child each year, and 2.0% of those surveyed said they have done these acts at least once while the child was growing up.

- A little less than 1% of the parents said they beat their child at least once a year, and 1% said they had beaten their child.

TABLE 3.2   Frequency of Parental Violence Toward Children

	Percentage of Occurrences in Past Year				Percentage of Occurrences Ever Reported
Violent Behavior	Once	Twice	More Than Twice	Total	
Threw something at child	1.5	0.7	0.9	3.1	4.5
Pushed, grabbed, or shoved child	5.8	7.5	14.9	28.2	33.6
Slapped or spanked child	8.1	8.5	39.1	55.7	74.6
Kicked, bit, or hit with fist	0.7	0.5	0.3	1.5	2.1
Hit or tried to hit child with something	2.4	2.0	5.3	9.7	14.4
Beat up child	0.3	0.1	0.2	0.6	1.0
Burned or scalded child	0.2	0.1	0.1	0.4	0.6
Threatened child with knife or gun	0.1	0.1	0	0.2	0.3
Used a knife or gun	0.1	0.1	0	0.2	0.2

SOURCE: Based on data from Gelles and Straus (1988).

- Two children in 1,000 faced a parent who threatened to use a gun or a knife during the survey year.

- Three children in 1,000 were threatened with a weapon by a parent while growing up. The same percentages held for children whose parents reported actually using a weapon.

Straus and Gelles (1988, 1990) also estimated the extent of abusive violence. Abusive violence was defined as acts that had a high probability of injuring the child (see Chapter 1 of this book). These included kicking, biting, punching, hitting or trying to hit a child with an object, beating up a child, burning or scalding, and threatening or using a gun or a knife:

- Slightly more than 20 parents in 1,000 (2.3%) engaged in one act of abusive violence during the year prior to the survey.

- Seven children in 1,000 were hurt as a result of an act of violence directed at them by a parent in the previous year.

Projecting the rate of abusive violence (23 per 1,000) to all children under the age of 18 who lived in the home means that 1.5 million children experience acts of abusive physical violence each year. Projecting the rate of injury (7 per 1,000) means that about 450,000 children are injured each year as a result of parental violence.

Acts of violence not only affect a large number of children, but on average they happen more than once a year. Straus and Gelles found that even the extreme forms of parental violence occur periodically and even regularly in the families where they occur. The median number of occurrences of acts of abusive violence was 4.5 times per year.

Straus and Gelles's (1988, 1990) study of violence toward children confirmed previous findings that violence does not end when the children grow up. More than 80% of the 3- to 9-year-olds were hit at least once a year (Wauchope & Straus, 1990). Two thirds of the preteens and young teenagers were hit, and more than one third of 15- to 17-year-olds were hit each year. Abusive acts of violence show no particular pattern with regard to age.

One of the important limitations to the survey conducted by Straus and his associates is that the survey measured only self-reports of violence toward children. Thus, the results indicate the rates of violence admitted to by parents, not the true level of violence toward children. In addition, the actual measure of violence and abuse was confined to a small number of violent acts. Sexual abuse and other forms of maltreatment were not measured in the study.

Nevertheless, the national study did yield valuable information regarding violence toward children and a projection of a rate of child abuse that was considerably higher than most other estimates of reported physical abuse. This is quite remarkable when one considers that Straus and his colleagues used a rather restricted list of abusive violent acts.

Sexual Abuse

The official report data cited above include the yearly incidence of cases of sexual abuse reported to state child welfare agencies. As with all forms of child maltreatment, reported cases are assumed to be underestimates of the true extent of sexual abuse. Unlike physical violence toward children, there has not yet been a self-report survey that attempts to measure the yearly incidence of sexual abuse. There have been a number of self-report prevalence studies. Peters, Wyatt, and Finkelhor (1986) report that estimates of prevalence range from 6% to 62% for females and from 3% to 31% for males. A 1985 national survey of 2,626 adult men and women found a life prevalence of sexual abuse reported by 27% of the women and 16% of the men surveyed (Finkelhor, Hotaling,

Lewis, & Smith, 1990). One of the important conclusions from this examination of the extent of sexual abuse is that males were victims of sexual abuse more often than is commonly assumed.

Psychological Abuse

Official report data are also assumed to underestimate the true extent of psychological abuse of children. There are few self-report surveys that attempt to assess the extent of psychological abuse or maltreatment. Using the Psychological Aggression scale from the Conflict Tactics Scales (Straus, 1979), Yvonne Vissing and her colleagues (Vissing et al., 1991) report that 63.4% of a national sample of 3,346 parents stated that they used at least one form of psychological aggression at least once in the previous year. This operationalization of psychological aggression is a rather broad definition of psychological maltreatment (items included "insulted or swore at the child," and "did or said something to spite the child").

Child Homicide

The U.S. Advisory Board on Child Abuse and Neglect (1995) estimated that 2,000 children under the age of 18 are killed by parents or caretakers each year. The board also suggests that this estimate is low. Philip McClain and his colleagues (McClain, Sacks, & Frohlke, 1993) report that abuse and neglect kill 5.4 out of every 100,000 children under 4 years of age, but this estimate is probably low as a result of misclassification of child deaths. McClain and his colleagues believe that some child homicides are mistakenly ruled accidents or cases of sudden infant death syndrome (SIDS) by medical examiners. A second estimate is that the rate of child death is 11.6 per 100,000 children under 4 years of age (U.S. Advisory Board on Child Abuse and Neglect, 1995).

The National Committee to Prevent Child Abuse and Neglect estimates that 1,271 children were killed by parents or caretakers in 1994, for a rate of 1.92 children per 100,000 (Weise & Daro, 1995).

Is Child Abuse Increasing?

Since the early 1960s, there has been a widespread belief that the rates of child abuse and violence toward children have been increasing. This

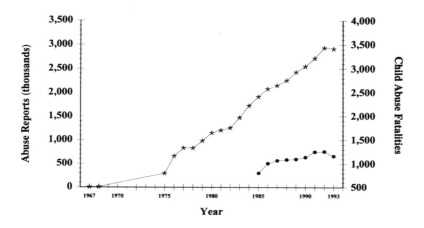

Figure 3.1. Reports of Child Abuse
SOURCE: Based on data from McCurdy and Daro (1993).
NOTE: ✶ = Abuse reports; ● = Child abuse fatalities.

belief has been partially supported by the fact that the number of cases of child abuse that are reported to social service agencies rose steadily between 1976 and 1992 (see Figure 3.1) (American Association for Protecting Children, 1989; U.S. Department of Health and Human Services, National Center on Child Abuse and Neglect, 1995). The rate of reported child maltreatment actually stayed even for the first time between 1992 and 1993.

The three National Center on Child Abuse and Neglect national surveys of the incidence of reported and recognized child abuse and neglect also found increases in reported child maltreatment. Countable cases of child maltreatment that have come to the attention of community professionals increased 66% between 1980 and 1986 and increased 105% between 1986 and 1993. There were significant increases in the incidence of physical and sexual abuse, with physical abuse increasing by 58% between 1980 and 1986 and by 102% between 1996 and 1993. Sexual abuse more than tripled between 1980 and 1986 and increased 126% between 1986 and 1993. The number of seriously injured children nearly quadrupled between 1986 and 1993.

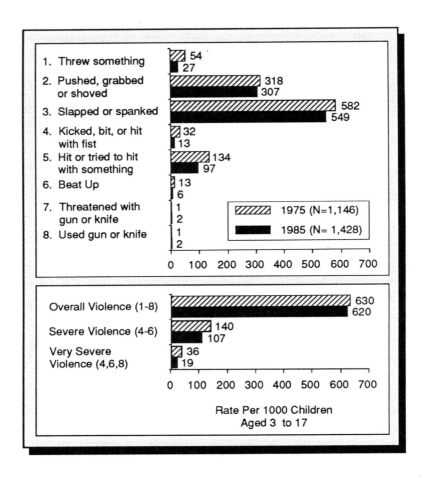

Figure 3.2. Parent-to-Child Violence: Comparison of Rates in 1975 and 1985

Straus and Gelles (1986) analyzed data from the Second National Family Violence Survey and found that parent reports of physical child abuse had *declined* 47% between 1976 and 1985 from 36 per 1,000 to 19 per 1,000 children (Figure 3.2). The rate of abusive violence toward Black children increased, but the change was not statistically significant (Hampton, Gelles, & Harrop, 1989).

More recent national surveys of parents' self-reports of violence toward children also find that the rates have either declined or remained stable. The National Committee to Prevent Child Abuse conducts an annual survey of parent attitudes and behaviors regarding child abuse prevention (Daro, 1995; Daro & Gelles, 1992). Parents' self-reports of spanking their children declined from 64% in 1988 to 47% in 1995. Reports of kicking, biting, or punching children or hitting or trying to hit children with objects remained about the same over the same period of time, at about 2%.

One likely explanation for the decrease in self-reports of violence toward children is that parents are becoming less candid because of the unacceptability of admitting to abusive behavior. Straus and Gelles (1986) recognized that changing attitudes about child abuse could be a plausible explanation for their findings. They also note, however, that the declining rate of child abuse is consistent with the changing character and structure of the American family, the improving economy (unemployment and inflation were lower in 1985 than in 1976), increased publicity about child abuse, and the rapid expansion of treatment and prevention programs for child abuse. The American family has become smaller in the past decade. Individuals are getting married later in life, having children later, having fewer children, and having fewer unwanted children. All these factors are consistent with lower risk of violence toward children. Given the expansion of both public awareness of child abuse and treatment and prevention programs, it would have been surprising and depressing to find that the rate of violence and abuse had increased.

Straus and Gelles attempt to resolve the apparent contradiction between their surveys and the results of the studies of officially reported and recognized child maltreatment. They note that an increase in the official report rate is not necessarily contradictory with a decline in the incidence rate. It is possible, Straus and Gelles explain, that an increase in the former (which is a proxy for the number of cases of abuse that are treated) could very well produce a decline in the later.

Who Are the Abusers and Who Is Abused?

Perhaps the most important and difficult questions to answer about violence and maltreatment toward children are, Who are the parents and caretakers most at risk of abusing their children, and which children are most at risk of being abused? There are a variety of factors that make these complex and difficult questions to answer. First, there are similarities and differences in the factors related to the different forms of violence and maltreatment. Although there are a few risk factors that are common to all the various forms of maltreatment, there are also important differences. For example, young age of the victim is strongly related to the risk of homicide, but not related to the risk of sexual abuse or physical punishment. Second, although it may be possible to find a risk factor for a specific form of abuse, abuse and maltreatment do not arise out of single factors; rather, there are complex and interacting characteristics of the offender, victim, and environment that combine to increase the risk of violence and abuse. Third, some factors may be related to the onset of violence and maltreatment, whereas other factors may be more strongly related to the continuation or even escalation of violence and abuse. Finally, even for single factors and specific forms of violence or abuse, there are often differing results depending on the study and source of data (National Research Council, 1993). Before looking at the risk factors for violence and abuse of children, I will briefly review the major sources of data on who are the likely abusers and victims.

Sources of Data

There are three sources of information about who abuses children and which children are the most likely to be abused. Each source of information has specific strengths and weaknesses. Sometimes the information from each source conflicts, and other times the findings are quite consistent. To be able to appreciate the claims and findings from each source, it is important to assess the relative strengths and weaknesses of the major types of information we have on the factors associated with child abuse.

One source of information about child abuse is clinical studies. Clinical studies depend on information collected by clinicians such as social workers, psychiatrists, psychologists, and marriage counselors. Clinicians can collect a considerable range of data with much detail because the clinicians see their patients over a period of time. However, clinical data typically are based on only a few cases (clinicians can only see a certain number of patients a week), and these cases are not randomly or representatively selected. Consequently, although data from clinical studies may be rich in descriptive information, one cannot generalize from these small numbers of cases to any larger population. Another limitation is that clinicians typically do not compare the information they obtain from cases of abuse to other families where abuse does not occur. Thus, they cannot be sure that the factors they find in the abusive families are unique to, or are even associated with, the acts of abuse.

A second source of information about child abuse is official reports. Each state has its own official reporting system and records. Official reports provide information about a large number of cases and describe a wide range of cases of abuse. However, the data speak more to the factors that lead someone to get reported for abuse than to what factors are actually associated with child abuse. There is a tendency for lower-income and lower-social-status individuals (e.g., ethnic minorities, in particular Blacks or some Spanish-speaking ethnic groups) to be overrepresented in these reports. Child abuse researchers have found considerable bias in the process of officially labeling and reporting child abuse (Hampton & Newberger, 1985). The physician Eli Newberger and his associates (Newberger et al., 1977) report that lower-class and minority children seen with injuries in a private hospital are more likely than middle- and upper-class children to be labeled abused. Patrick Turbett and Richard O'Toole (1980), using an experimental design, found that physicians are more likely to label minority children and lower-class children as abused (a mock case was presented to the physicians, with the injury remaining constant and the race or class of the child varied).

The third source of information is survey data collected from representative samples of a given population. Unfortunately, there have been very few surveys conducted on child abuse. Two such studies are the ones conducted by Straus and Gelles (Gelles & Straus, 1988; Straus et al., 1980). Self-report surveys also have limitations. First, and most obvious, respondents may be unwilling to report engaging in behavior that is thought to be deviant. Second, respondents may fail to remember engaging in violent or abusive behavior or may not remember being hit, maltreated, or sexually abused (Williams, 1994).

Our discussion of factors associated with child abuse draws from all three sources of information. Where the three sources agree we find the most powerful explanations of what child factors and parent factors are related to the abuse of children.

Child Factors

The very youngest children appear to be at the greatest risk of being physically abused and killed (Fergusson, Fleming, & O'Neil, 1972; Gil, 1970; Johnson, 1974; U.S. Advisory Board on Child Abuse and Neglect, 1995). Forty-one percent of children killed by parents and caretakers are under 1 year of age, and only 10% of child fatalities were children older than 4 years of age (McClain et al., 1993; Levine, Compaan, & Freeman, 1994, 1995). Not only are young children physically more fragile and thus more susceptible to injury, but their vulnerability makes them more likely to be reported and diagnosed as abused when injured.

Older children are underreported as victims of physical abuse. Adolescent victims may be considered delinquent or ungovernable, and thus thought of as contributing to their own victimization.

Girls aged 10 to 12 are found to be the most likely victims of sexual abuse at the hands of adults (Finkelhor, 1984), and children aged 3 to 5 are most likely to be sexually victimized by other children (English, 1993).

Early research suggested that there were a number of factors that raise the risk of a child being abused. Low-birth-weight babies (Parke & Collmer, 1975); premature children (Elmer, 1967; Newberger et al., 1977; Parke & Collmer, 1975; Steele & Pollack, 1974); and handicapped, retarded, or developmentally disabled children (Friederich & Boriskin, 1976; Gil, 1970; Steinmetz, 1978b) were all described as being at greater risk of being abused by their parents or caretakers. A recent study found that children with physical or emotional disabilities were twice as likely to be physically abused and $1\frac{1}{2}$ times as likely to be sexually abused as nondisabled children ("Study of High Risk," 1992).

However, recent reviews of studies that examine the characteristics of children who are abused call into question many of these findings (Starr, 1988). One of the reasons for the difference in the findings on factors related to a child's vulnerability and the risk of abuse is that parental and social factors, such as poverty, isolation, and socioeconomic status, are related both to the risk of having a child born prematurely and with a low birth weight *and* to the risk of abusing a child (Leventhal, Horwitz, Rude, & Steir, 1993). Another problem is that few investigators use appropriate comparison groups.

Overall, child characteristics may play only a minor role in the initiation of violence and abuse, but could play a more important role in the maintenance, persistence, or escalation of violence and maltreatment. As a result of being abused or neglected, children may exhibit behaviors such as aggression, provocative behavior, or withdrawal that could lead to more abuse. Sexually abused children may develop or learn sexualized behaviors that put them at risk of continued abuse by the same perpetrator or new abuse by different perpetrators (Ammerman, 1991; Dodge, Bates, & Pettit, 1990; Friederich, 1988).

Parent and Caretaker Factors

Individual traits. As I discussed in the first chapter, early clinical and psychiatric studies of abuse reported that mental illness and psychosis were common among abusers. Some studies suggested that parents who score low on intelligence tests are more likely to abuse their children (Smith, Honigsberger, & Smith, 1973; Wright, 1971). However, most students of child abuse have found little difference between abusers and nonabusers in terms of intellectual ability (see, e.g., Starr, 1982). Although a small percentage of parents and caretakers who maltreat their children can be reliably diagnosed as having a psychiatric disorder, most people who abuse or maltreat children do not have a specifically diagnosable psychiatric disorder (National Research Council, 1993).

The search for individual traits associated with violence and abuse of children has identified numerous personality characteristics related to physical abuse, including depression, immaturity, and impulsiveness. The three most important personality attributes of physical abusers are depression, anxiety, and antisocial behavior (National Research Council, 1993).

Similarly, psychiatric profiles of sex offenders tend to find the presence of antisocial personality disorders (Conte, 1984; Lanning, 1992; Prentky, 1990).

Another pervasive notion is that alcohol or drug misuse, such as heroin, cocaine, and crack cocaine, are associated with abuse (Fontana, 1973; Martin & Walters, 1982; Wertham, 1972; Young, 1964). Reviews of the relationship between alcohol, alcohol abuse, and child abuse concluded that if alcohol is involved in child abuse, its influence does not appear to be strong or pervasive, but rather restricted to certain subgroups of abusers or types of abuse (Gelles, 1993; Leonard & Jacob, 1988). Researchers note that alcohol probably plays no direct role in abuse; rather, drinking and drunkenness can be used as a socially acceptable excuse for mistreating children (Gelles, 1993; Straus et al., 1980). Although substance abuse is also highly associated with child maltreatment, it is also unlikely that the substances themselves produce the abusive behavior. Heroin, cocaine, and crack are used in a context of poverty and family and community disorganization. Thus, drug abuse, although an important factor in maltreatment, is related to abuse through a complex series of mechanisms and processes.

A final individual factor sometimes found in abusive parents is that they tend to have unrealistically high expectations for their children. It is not uncommon for a 6-month-old infant to be admitted into a hospital for injuries inflicted by a parent who was angry because the child was not toilet trained. Research results, however, are inconsistent and it does not appear that abusive parents are markedly deviant in their knowledge of children's normal developmental milestones (Starr, 1988). Raymond Starr (1988) explains that even if parents have adequate knowledge of child development, they may not apply such knowledge to their child-rearing practices.

Conventional wisdom suggests that people who abuse their children must be crazy or suffer from some kind of personality or character disorder. Although there is no specific psychiatric disorder that is common to abusive parents nor a precise personality profile that distinguishes violent and abusive parents from other parents, there are certain personality and individual characteristics that are commonly found among parents and caretakers who maltreat their children. These traits, however, do not exist in isolation. They may be the result of stresses such as poverty, unemployment, stress, or prior victimization, or they could be compounded by these factors.

Family factors. Single parents and stepparents have been thought to be at high risk of abusing their children. Official report data and survey data find that single parents are overrepresented among abusers (American Humane Association, 1984; Gelles, 1989; Sack, Mason, & Higgins, 1985; Wilson, Daly, & Weghorst, 1980). Two explanations have been offered for why single parents are more likely to abuse their children. First, single parents often have to meet the demands of child rearing without the assistance of another adult. Second, single parents are more likely to live in poverty than dual-caretaker parents. Our own analysis of the data from the Second National Family Violence Survey found that single parents were more likely to hit and abuse their children. The greater risk was not a function of single parents having to raise their children alone—single parents alone had the same rates of violence and abuse as single parents who lived with other adults. The risk of violence in single-parent homes was a function of the high rate of poverty that single parents—mostly single mothers—must endure (Gelles, 1989).

The wicked stepparent is a staple of children's literature, and students of child abuse have often found stepparents to be overrepresented in clinical and official report data on child maltreatment (American Humane Association, 1976; Daly & Wilson, 1980, 1981, 1985, 1987, 1988a, 1988b; Gil, 1970; Giles-Sims & Finkelhor, 1984; Wilson & Daly, 1987). Survey data, however, do not support the claim that stepparents are more violent or abusive than genetic parents (Gelles & Harrop, 1991). However, stepparents and caretakers who are not biologically related to their children are at greater risk of killing their children or sexually abusing children in their care (Daly & Wilson, 1988b; Gordon, 1989; Gordon & Creighton, 1988).

Demographic Factors

Clinical observations, official reports, and survey data find that mothers are more likely to abuse their children than fathers. Although the difference between men and women is not large, what difference does exist is probably due to factors other than gender. Mothers tend to spend more time with children, especially younger children and infants. Irrespective of the time actually spent with children, in our society mothers are considered more responsible for the children's behavior than are fathers. Leslie Margolin (1992) explains that most examinations of sex of offender and child maltreatment fail to actually examine the different levels of responsibility males and females have for child care and child rearing. When the level of responsibility for child care is controlled, for instance, comparing abuse committed by male and female baby-sitters (Margolin, 1991), or comparing abuse by single parents (Gelles, 1989), males are more likely to be physical abusers than are females. Although there are female perpetrators of sexual abuse, both official report data and self-report surveys are consistent in finding that the majority of sexual abusers are males (Finkelhor, 1987).

Research on parents' age and child maltreatment is somewhat inconsistent. Some researchers have found that young adults are more likely to abuse their children, whereas other studies find no relationship between age and maltreatment, or find that the effects of age are really a function of social class (National Research Council, 1993). However, when the age of the mother at the time she gave birth to the child is assessed, the younger mothers tend to have higher rates of physical abuse (Connelley & Straus, 1992; Kinard & Klerman, 1980).

Official reports of child abuse overrepresent African Americans in comparison to the percentage of African Americans in the general population (U.S. Department of Health and Human Services, National Center on Child Abuse and Neglect, 1995). Latinos are not over-represented in official reports, whereas Asian Americans and Pacific Islanders are reported at rates lower than their representation in the population. The three national surveys of the incidence of reported and recognized child maltreatment found that the rates of maltreatment among African Americans were no greater than the rates among other racial groups (Burgdorf, 1980; National Center on Child Abuse and Neglect, 1988, 1996). To complicate the assessment of the relationship between race and ethnicity and child abuse, the two national surveys of family violence found differing results. The First National Family Violence Survey found that the rates of violence and abuse of children were essentially the same in African American and white families (Straus et al., 1980). In 1985, the rate of overall violence, a measure of physical punishment, remained the same in African American and white homes, but the rate of abusive violence toward African American children was about twice the rate for abusive violence toward white children (Hampton et al., 1989). Violence and severe violence toward children was higher in Latino families than in non-Latino white families (Straus & Smith, 1990). This higher rate of violence toward children in Latino families was not a function of poverty, youthfulness, urbanization, or other demographic factors. Thus, ethnicity, in and of itself, is not related to child maltreatment.

Economic Factors

Although child maltreatment is reported across all social classes, it is disproportionately reported among poor families. This does not mean that all or even most poor families abuse their children. Low-income families have the highest rates of physical abuse and are the most likely to be reported. Those in the lowest income groups have 2 or 3 times greater rates of abuse than upper-income families. Again, it is important to remember that abuse does occur in all economic groups, but it is *most likely* to happen among the poor or disadvantaged (National Research Council, 1993). The exception is sexual abuse (Finkelhor, 1987).

Because low income is related to abuse, we should not be surprised that other socioeconomic factors are also related. A person's occupation has a significant effect on the chances of abuse occurring, because occupation is a predictor of income. Blue-collar workers have higher rates of the use of physical punishment and abuse (Kohn, 1977; Steinmetz, 1971; Straus et al., 1980). This could be the result of the lower-income blue-collar workers' earnings compared with those of white-collar workers, or it could be because blue-collar workers are more accepting of the use of corporal punishment. Because blue-collar work requires following orders and deferring to authority, blue-collar workers tend to believe that their children should also follow orders and defer to authority.

Children whose fathers are unemployed or work part-time are more likely to be abused compared with children of fathers with full-time jobs (National Research Council, 1993). There was a time when some child abuse researchers thought that working mothers were more likely to abuse their children. However, research finds that whether a mother works or does not work has no direct effect on her chances of abusing her child (Gelles & Hargreaves, 1981).

Stress

Given that poverty and unemployment are linked to violence toward children, it is also assumed that other forms of personal and family stress are associated with violence and abuse. A number of researchers have found that overall levels of stressful events in a family and particular stressful events, such as a new baby, presence of a handicapped person in the home, illness, death of a family member, and child care problems, are linked to higher rates of abuse and violence (Egeland, Breitenbucher, & Rosenberg, 1980; Straus & Kaufman Kantor, 1987). It is generally thought that the risk of child abuse is highest in families with the largest number of children and with closely spaced children (Belsky, 1993; Starr, 1988).

Social Isolation

Social isolation has been considered an important risk factor for all forms of child maltreatment, including child sexual abuse. Much of the data supporting the notion about social isolation have been clinical or anecdotal. Moreover, researchers have not teased out whether social isolation is a cause or consequence of child maltreatment (Polansky, Chalmers, Buttenweiser, & Williams, 1981; Polansky, Gaudin, & Kilpatrick, 1992). Involvement in a social network of friends and family is generally thought to be a protective factor that prevents stress, poverty, or other factors from leading to child abuse and neglect (Garbarino, 1977). Isolated parents who do not have much in the way of social support may maltreat their children when stresses or other problems cannot be managed. On the other hand, parents may maltreat their children and then be isolated by friends and family as a result of their deviant behaviors and the other factors that may be associated with abuse, such as alcohol or drug problems.

Intergenerational Transmission
of Violence and Abuse

No finding regarding child abuse and violence toward children has been more consistently reported in the literature than the finding that persons who observed family violence, were victims of violence, or were exposed to high levels of family violence in childhood are more likely to be abusers (for reviews of this literature, see National Research Council, 1993; Widom, 1989b). I have already provided the caution (see Chapter 1) that this does not mean that all victims of childhood violence will grow up to be abusers, nor are people who have no violence in their childhood experience immune to violent behavior as adults.

Joan Kaufman and Edward Zigler (1987, 1993) reviewed the research that tested the theory of the intergenerational transmission of violence hypothesis (also referred to as the cycle of violence). Kaufman and Zigler reported that most papers on this topic still base the observations on case studies of children treated in hospital emergency rooms. A second source of data are agency record studies, which, according to Kaufman and Zigler, have limited value for testing the cycle-of-violence hypothesis. The third source are self-report studies. Reviewing the self-report studies that examined the cycle-of-violence hypothesis, Kaufman and Zigler found that the rate of intergenerational transmission ranged from 18% to 70%. They concluded that the best estimate of the rate of intergenerational transmission appears to be 30% (plus or minus 5%). Based on this estimate, Kaufman and Zigler conclude that it is time for the intergenerational myth to be set aside and for researchers to cease asking, Do abused children become abusive parents? and ask, instead, Under what conditions is the transmission of abuse likely to occur?

Kaufman and Zigler's (1987, 1993) conclusion appears to be as sweeping and insupportable as the claim that *all* abused children will grow up to be abusive. Although the best estimate of a rate of 30% intergenerational transmission is quite a bit less than half of abused children, the rate is considerably more than the rate of between 2% and 4% of abuse found in the general population.

Three studies provide some insights into the intergenerational transmission of abuse. Rosemary Hunter and her colleagues (Hunter, Kilstrom, Kraybill, & Loda, 1978) studied mothers of premature or ill newborns and found that 10 out of their sample of 255 were reported for substantiated incidents of abuse or neglect during the child's first year of life. Nine of the 10 mothers reported a family history of abuse, whereas only 17% of the comparison mothers reported such a history. Of the 49 families in which a parent reported being abused as a child, 9 abused their infants (Hunter & Kilstrom, 1979). Byron Egeland, Deborah Jacobvitz, and L. Alan Sroufe (1988) note that this rate will increase as the infants are followed beyond the first year.

Egeland and his colleagues (Egeland, Jacobvitz, & Papatola, 1987; Egeland et al., 1988) have conducted a prospective study of the intergenerational transmission of violence. They followed a sample of 160 high-risk, low-income mothers. In this prospective study, 70% of the parents who were identified independently as having experienced child abuse were observed to maltreat or provide minimally adequate care. Egeland et al. (1988) report that those mothers who were able to break the cycle of violence were significantly more likely to have received emotional support from a nonabusive adult during childhood, participated in therapy during any period in their lives, and had a nonabusive, more stable, emotionally supportive and satisfying relationship with a mate.

A third study conducted by Ellen Herrenkohl, Roy Herrenkohl, and Lori Toedler (1983) found that 47% of the parents who were abused as children abused their own children. This percentage is significantly higher than the percentage for the nonabused parents.

In summary, there have been a few controlled studies that actually test the public perception that abused children grow up to be abusive parents. Most studies conclude that the majority of abused children do not go on to be abusive parents. However, a violent background is an important contributor to the likelihood that a person will be violent toward a child.

Summary

From the preceding discussion of factors that are associated with violence toward children and child maltreatment, it should be quite clear that there is no single factor that leads a parent to abuse a child. Characteristics of the child, parent, family, social situation, and community influence which children are abused and under what conditions. Moreover, some factors are related to sexual abuse, but not physical abuse; some are related to neglect and not other forms of maltreatment; and some factors, such as history of being abused, may be related to all forms of maltreatment. In addition, some factors may be related to the less dangerous manifestations of maltreatment, whereas other factors or combination of factors may be related to the more dangerous and life-threatening forms of abuse. Rebecca Hegar and her colleagues (Hegar, Zuravin, & Orme, 1994) reviewed the literature on predictors of severe and fatal child abuse and concluded that the one consistent predictor of severity of injury was the young age of the child. There was less consistent support for the conclusions that boys, children of color, and victims of male perpetrators may be at increased risk of injury.

Figure 3.3 is a social-psychological summarizing of the factors associated with child abuse. This summary should not be confused with a causal explanation of violence and abuse. Chapter 6 will review the theories and explanation of family violence in detail.

We can safely say at this point that there are multiple causes of child abuse. Because there are multiple and not single causes, this has a profound effect on the process of identifying and treating abuse. Obviously, a clinical assessment of suspected abuse cannot simply look for a single factor to signal whether a child has been abused. It is not sufficient to know that the parents were abused. An assessment of only one parent will not be sufficient, nor will just an examination of the parent's home and

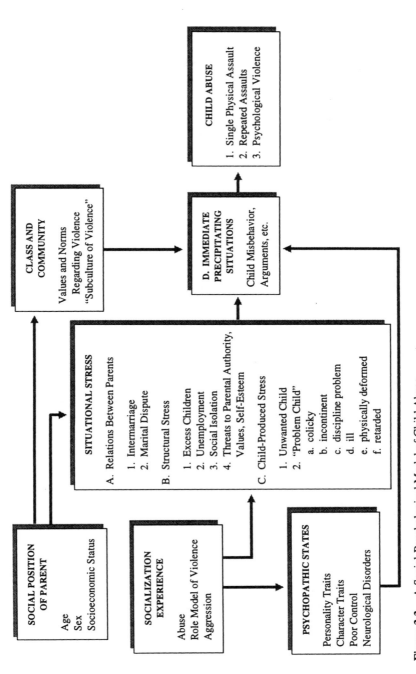

Figure 3.3. A Social-Psychological Model of Child Abuse

SOURCE: Gelles (1973); reprinted with permission from the *American Journal of Orthopsychiatry*, copyright 1973, American Orthopsychiatric Asociation, Inc.

65

lifestyle. Many a social worker has misdiagnosed a suspected injury by relying too much on how neat the child's home was or was not. As we will see in the concluding chapter of this book, prevention and treatment need to be based on a model of multiple causes. The characteristics of the child, parents, family, and social situation are all important in understanding and helping the abusive family.

Consequences of Child Abuse and Neglect

The consequences of child abuse and neglect can be devastating. Researchers and clinicians have documented physical, psychological, cognitive, and behavioral consequences of physical abuse, psychological abuse, sexual abuse, and neglect. Physical damage can range from death, brain damage, and permanent disabilities to minor bruises and scrapes. The psychological consequences can range from lowered sense of self-worth to severe psychiatric disorders, including dissociative states. Cognitive problems range from severe organic brain disorders to reduced attention and minor learning disorders. Maltreated children's behavioral problems can include severe violent and criminal behavior and suicide as well as inability to relate to peers (National Research Council, 1993). Not only are there consequences for the victims of abuse and neglect, but there are consequences for their families, communities, and society in general. For example, Deborah Daro (1988) developed a cost estimate for child maltreatment by calculating the number of child abuse reports received, what percentage were substantiated, and what percentage actually received various types of services, including foster care. Daro estimated that the immediate cost of hospitalizing abused and neglected children was $20 million annually, rehabilitation and special education cost $7 million, and foster care costs were $460 million. In addition, there would be short-term education, juvenile court, and private therapy costs. Longer-term costs included $14.8 million for juvenile court and detention costs, $646 million for long-term foster care, and future lost earnings of abused and neglected children of between $658 million to $1.3 billion. Jack Westman (1994) extrapolated Daro's costs for 1994 and included estimates for hospitalization, rehabilitation and special education, foster care, social services case management, and court expenses. His cost estimate was between $8.4 and $32.3 billion each year, based on a range of $12,174 to $46,870 per maltreated child per year.

As severe and significant as the consequences of child abuse and neglect are, it is also important to point out that the majority of children who are abused and neglected do not show signs of extreme disturbance. Despite having been physically abused, psychologically abused, or sexually abused, many children have effective coping abilities and thus are able to deal with their problems better than other maltreated children. There are a number of protective factors that insulate children from the effects of maltreatment. These include high intelligence and good scholastic attainment; temperament; cognitive appraisal of events, that is, how the child views the maltreatment; having a relationship with a significant person; and the types of interventions, including placement outside of the home (National Research Council, 1993).

It is also important to note that even when there are major negative consequences of maltreatment, there may be other factors that lead to the poor outcomes. The same factors that are related to child maltreatment— poverty, family structure, occurrence of spouse abuse in the home, alcohol or drug problems of the parents—may also contribute to the psychological, cognitive, and behavioral outcomes for maltreated children. In addition, the child's age and developmental status at the time of the maltreatment may influence the outcomes of the maltreatment experience.

The consequences of child abuse and neglect differ by the age of the child. During childhood, some of the major consequences of maltreatment include problematic school performance and lowered attention to social cues. Researchers have found that children whose parents were "psychologically unavailable" functioned poorly across a wide range of psychological, cognitive, and developmental areas (Egeland & Sroufe, 1981). Physical aggression, antisocial behavior, and juvenile delinquency are among the most consistently documented consequences of abuse in adolescence and adulthood (Aber, Allen, Carlson, & Cicchetti, 1990; Dodge et al., 1990; Widom, 1989a, 1989b, 1991). Evidence is more suggestive that maltreatment increases the risk of alcohol and drug problems (National Research Council, 1993). Research on the consequences of sexual abuse finds that inappropriate sexual behavior, such as frequent and overt sexual stimulation and inappropriate sexual overtures to other children, are commonly found among victims of sexual abuse (Kendall-Tackett, Williams, & Finkelhor, 1993). Cathy Spatz Widom (1995) has found that people who were sexually abused during childhood are at higher risk of arrest for committing crimes as adults, including sex crimes, compared with people who did not suffer sexual abuse. However, this risk is no greater than the risk of arrest for victims of other childhood maltreatment, with one exception. Victims of sexual abuse are more likely to be arrested for prostitution than are victims of other maltreatment.

In summary, the legacy of child abuse is more than the physical scars that children carry with them. Research indicates that there are emotional and developmental scars as well. Family violence can also spill out onto the street. Moreover, there is the issue of quality of life—the day-to-day effect of violence and its threat on children and the entire family.

Notes

1. All the studies of college students used "convenience" samples. Questionnaires were filled out by students enrolled in introductory sociology or psychology classes. Because the samples were not representative, the results cannot be generalized to campuses where the research was conducted. Because college students are not representative of all 18-year-olds, the results cannot be generalized to all high school seniors. Nevertheless, the results from a number of different campuses are quite consistent and suggest that even in fairly affluent, white, middle-class homes, violence toward children extends well into children's adolescence.

2. Prior to 1992, state reports of child maltreatment were collected and analyzed by the American Association for Protecting Children (1988, 1989). During 1987, the last year the survey was conducted, 2,178,384 children were reported to state agencies for suspected child abuse and neglect. Of these, it is estimated that 686,000 reports were substantiated by the state child protective services agencies.

3. A *victim* is defined as a child whose case was either substantiated or indicated after an investigation by a child protective services agency. *Substantiated* is defined as a type of investigation disposition that is used when the allegation of maltreatment was supported or founded by state law or state policy. This is considered the highest level of finding by a state agency. *Indicated* is defined as a type of investigation that concludes that maltreatment could not be substantiated under state law or policy but there is reason to suspect that the child may have been maltreated or was at risk of maltreatment (U.S. Department of Health and Human Services, National Center on Child Abuse and Neglect, 1995).

4. These data are based on reports from 37 states.

DISCUSSION QUESTIONS

1. What techniques have been used to measure the extent of child abuse in the United States? Discuss the advantages and disadvantages of each technique.

2. Are poor people more likely to abuse their children, to be correctly or incorrectly labeled child abusers, or both?

3. What are the implications for clinicians, who must diagnose and treat child abuse, of the conclusion that there are multiple factors associated with the abuse of children?

SUGGESTED ASSIGNMENTS

1. Observe how parents discipline children in a public place, such as in a toy store or fast food restaurant. Develop a "coding" form by which you can keep track of how frequently parents use physical punishment to discipline their children. Try to observe in different locations and see if the setting, situation, and social class of the parents influence their public behavior.

2. Contact your local child welfare agency (state, city, or local). Ask for the official tally of child abuse reports for the past 10 or even 20 years. See whether you can see any trends in the changes.

4

THE "APPROPRIATE" VICTIMS

Women

The scene is the emergency room of a children's hospital. This evening, like so many before and so many that would follow, the staff is hovering over a suspected case of child abuse. A 3-year-old boy is being examined. He has a number of cuts and abrasions, but what catches everyone's attention is the outline of a hand on the side of his face. A young physician suddenly turns to the boy's mother and yells at her. "How could you do this?" he begins, until he finally concludes, "I will see that your child is taken away from you and this will never happen again!"

The senior social worker on duty moves in and takes the physician aside. Beginning with the obvious statement, "You seem to be upset," the social worker then asks the doctor if he can describe the mother. "Tell me what she looks like," the social worker asks. The physician, a little calmer, could offer only the briefest description. "Come back with me," the social worker offers, and they return again to the mother and the child. "How did you lose your front teeth?" the social worker asks the mother. "Oh, my husband knocked them out last week," the mother replies in a flat, emotionless tone. Turning to the doctor, the social worker notes, "You have two victims here."

Wife abuse was publicly recognized as a social problem some 10 years after child abuse had received widespread public attention. And yet, until quite recently, women were overlooked as victims of family violence, both by physicians and the public. Although most states have revised their family and criminal laws to deal with domestic violence, women who are abused are generally ignored or treated less seriously than child victims of family violence. Ten years ago, when asked why the U.S. Senate was not holding hearings on wife abuse, as it did for child abuse, a senator replied sarcastically that eliminating wife abuse "would take all the fun out of marriage." A district court judge in an eastern city, after hearing a wife present her case against her husband's violence, leaned over the bench and smiled at the husband and said, "If I were you, I would have hit her too."

Much has changed in the past 10 years. Even if U.S. senators and state judges still think like the two cited above, they are much more reluctant to publicly voice such opinions and attitudes. There has been a significant change in public awareness as well as action and legislation around the issue of violence against women. As noted in Chapter 2, the Violence Against Women Act established an office within the U.S. Department of Justice on the issue of violence against women and provided funding to assist state support of social services and criminal justice reforms aimed at reducing violence against women. The federal government funds a National Resource Center on Domestic Violence and has provided funding for a National Domestic Violence Hotline (1-800-799-SAFE) to provide 24-hour counseling, problem-solving techniques, and referrals for battered women and their families from across the country. The American Medical Association, under the leadership of former president Robert McAfee, has focused considerable attention on the problem of domestic violence and the need to provide physicians and medical personnel training around diagnosis, treatment, and referrals for victims of domestic violence.

As I noted in Chapter 2, there are abundant historical and cross-cultural data to support the claim that women are the "appropriate" victims of domestic violence. In fact, some researchers have gone so far as to claim that the "marriage license is a hitting license." Lately, we have learned that it does not take a license to hit. The chapter begins by reviewing courtship or dating violence. Next, I consider the extent of violence toward women and what factors are associated with woman battery. The following section takes on the most pervasive myth in the study of women abuse; if women stay with assaultive men, then they, the women, must like the violence. This section reviews the reasons why some women stay in violent relationships and why others leave. I also examine research that looks at women who stayed with men and the violence stopped. Finally, the chapter concludes with a discussion of men as victims of domestic violence.

Courtship Violence

The virtues of romantic love, a phenomenon considered synonymous with American dating patterns, have been extolled in poems, songs, romance novels, television soap operas, and folklore. Sadly, along with the moonlight cruises, the first kiss, the flirtations, and affections is also the startling fact that violence is very much a part of American dating patterns. Studies that examined the possibility of violence in dating and courtship found that between 10% and 67% of dating relationships involve violence (Sugarman & Hotaling, 1989). Researchers who have examined dating violence among college students estimate that, on average, about one in four current relationships could be classified as aggressive (Riggs, O'Leary, & Breslin, 1990). As in other violent intimate relationships, the milder forms of violence (pushing, slapping, shoving) are the most common. However, severe violence is surprisingly common. Researchers have found that the rate of severe violence among dating couples ranged from about 1% each year to 27% (Arias, Samois, & O'Leary, 1987; Lane & Gwartney-Gibbs, 1985; Lloyd & Emery, 1994; Makepeace, 1981). This violence also is a pattern among couples of high school age. Twelve percent of high school students who date reported experiencing a form of dating violence (Henton, Cate, Koval, Lloyd, & Christopher, 1983). One victim reported having a gun or knife used on her, whereas two persons said they used a gun or a knife on a dating partner. Physical violence is not the only form of aggression and abuse that occurs in dating. National samples of college women reveal that nearly two in five have experienced an actual rape, attempted rape, or have been coerced into intercourse against their will (Koss & Cook, 1993; Koss, Gidycz, & Wisniewski, 1987).[1]

Perhaps the saddest and most revealing finding from the research on dating violence is how the individuals perceive the violence. In a study conducted by the sociologist June Henton and her colleagues (1983), more than one fourth of the victims, and 3 of 10 offenders, interpreted the violence as a sign of love. This is a sobering extension of the elementary school yard scenario where the young girl recipient of a push, shove, or hit thinks that it means the boy who hit her likes her. Rather than the violent episodes shattering the romantic images held by the participants, one gets the impression that violence serves to protect the romantic illusions of dating or vice versa. Indeed, 40% of the women who reported that they were sexually victimized in a dating relationship reported having sex again with the man who raped them (Koss & Cook, 1993). Victims of dating violence sometimes take the blame for helping to start the violence and are reluctant to blame their partners for the abuse. In addition, victims of courtship violence and sexual assault are reluctant to tell others about their experiences. If they do talk about the violence, it is with peers and not parents or teachers.

It is quite clear from the studies of courtship violence and date and acquaintance rape that many of the patterns we find in marital violence emerge long before a person gets married. One study that interviewed battered women who had sought shelter found that 51% of these women said that they had been physically abused in a dating relationship (Roscoe & Bernaske, 1985). If the marriage license is not a hitting license, then we must focus more closely on the relationship between the social norms about romance, intimacy, and violence.

Extent of Violence Against Women

The pattern of courtship violence helps us to understand some important things about domestic violence. First, as noted previously, there is a tendency on the part of many victims and offenders to view the violence as appropriate. Second, female victims are reluctant to blame their partners for the violence and tend to say that both persons were to blame for the abuse. Third, victims might blame themselves ("I asked for it"). Last, there is a tendency not to talk about the violence with family or friends.

Because violence between husbands and wives was traditionally hidden in the home, there has been, until quite recently, a general lack of awareness of the seriousness and extent of the problem. Whereas mandatory reporting laws for child abuse and neglect were enacted in every state in the late 1960s and early 1970s, only a handful of states today have mandatory reporting laws for domestic violence. Some hospitals record the number of women treated for spousal violence, and most police departments keep a rough record of domestic disturbance calls. Even without official records on spouse abuse, a variety of data sources suggest that domestic violence is far more extensive than commonly realized.

Homicide

Homicide is the one aspect of spousal violence on which official data are available. Researchers generally report that homicides between family members account for between 20% and 40% of all murders (Curtis, 1974). Nearly 700 husbands and boyfriends are killed by their wives and girlfriends each year, whereas more than 1,400 wives and girlfriends are slain by their husbands or boyfriends (U.S. Department of Justice, 1995).

National Crime Victimization Survey Data

There are as yet no national surveys of reported spouse abuse that collect state data in the same manner that child maltreatment report data have been collected and analyzed; thus, most of the data on the extent of violence toward women and between partners come from self-report surveys.

One source of self-report survey data is the U.S. Department of Justice's National Crime Victimization Survey (NCVS). The NCVS collects data from a nationally representative sample of some 60,000 households each year. Violent crimes included in the NCVS include rape, robbery, and assault (but not murder). The U.S. Bureau of Justice Statistics published a number of reports on violence against women prior to 1994 (Bachman, 1994; U.S. Department of Justice, 1980, 1984, 1994a), but these studies were based on NCVSs that did not specifically ask or cue respondents to the issue of violence between intimates. The Bureau of Justice Statistics redesigned the study and began administering the new survey in 1992. According to data from the redesigned survey, 9 women in 1,000, or 1 million women each year, experience violence at the hands of an intimate

(Bachman & Saltzman, 1995). The rate of violent victimization at the hands of a stranger was 7.4 per 1,000.

National Survey of Marital Violence

The NCVS, although redesigned, is a study of criminal victimization and still does not employ a precise measure of domestic violence. Thus, it is likely that this study underestimates the actual extent of intimate violence.

The same national studies that examined child abuse (see the previous chapter) also examined marital violence. Together with Murray Straus, I interviewed a nationally representative sample of 2,143 family members in 1976 and a nationally representative sample of 6,002 individuals in 1985. Using the same Conflict Tactics Scales (Straus, 1979), we examined violence between husbands and wives.

- In 16% of the homes surveyed in 1985, some kind of violence between spouses had occurred in the year prior to the survey. More than one in four (28%) of the couples reported marital violence at some point in their marriages.

As with violence toward children and courtship violence, the milder forms of violence were the most common (see Table 4.1):

- In terms of those acts of violence that would be considered wife beating (i.e., had the high potential of causing an injury), the National Family Violence Survey revealed that 34 per 1,000 American women, or 1 woman in 22, was a victim of abusive violence during the 12-month period prior to the interview in 1985. This rate means that at least 1.8 million women each year experience severe violence or wife beating. (Note: The difference between the National Family Violence Survey, 34 per 1,000 equaled 1.8 million, and the NCVS, 9 per 1,000 equaled 1 million, is that the National Family Violence Survey projected the rate to married women or women who lived with men, and the NCVS rate was projected to all women 12 years of age or older.)

Wife beating is a pattern, not a single event in most violent households. On average, a woman who is a victim of wife abuse is abused three times each year.

TABLE 4.1 Frequency of Marital Violence: Comparison of Husband and Wife Violence Rates (in percentages)

Violent Behavior	Incidence Rate		Mean (frequency)		Median (frequency)	
	Husband	Wife	Husband	Wife	Husband	Wife
1. Threw something at spouse	2.9	4.6	3.7	2.7	1.5	1.0
2. Pushed, grabbed, or shoved spouse	9.6	9.1	2.9	3.1	2.0	2.0
3. Slapped spouse	3.1	4.4	2.8	2.7	1.0	1.0
4. Kicked, bit, or hit with fist	1.5	2.5	3.9	2.9	1.5	1.0
5. Hit or tried to hit spouse with something	1.9	3.1	3.6	3.3	1.2	1.1
6. Beat up spouse	0.8	0.5	4.2	5.7	2.0	2.0
7. Choked spouse	0.7	0.4	1.9	2.9	1.0	1.0
8. Threatened spouse with knife or gun	0.4	0.6	4.3	2.0	1.8	1.1
9. Used a knife or gun	0.2	0.2	18.6	12.9	1.5	4.0
Overall violence (Items 1-9)	21.3	12.4	5.4	6.1	1.5	2.5
Wife beating and husband beating (Items 4-9)	3.4	4.8	5.2	5.4	1.5	1.5

SOURCE: Based on data from Gelles and Straus (1988).

Sexual Violence and Marital Rape

Just as violence is not the only form of abuse children experience, physical abuse is not the only form of victimization women endure. The sociologist Diana Russell (1980) interviewed a representative sample of 930 women in San Francisco. Of the 644 married women in the sample, 12% said they had been raped by their own husbands. The sociologists David Finkelhor and Kersti Yllö (1985) interviewed 323 Boston-area women for their book *License to Rape: Sexual Abuse of Wives.* Ten percent of the women said they had been forced to have sex with their husbands or partners. Last, Murray Straus and I asked a nationally representative sample of women if their partners ever tried or forced them to have sexual relations by using physical force. The results indicate that 50 women per 1,000 have husbands who attempt to force them to have sex each year, and an additional 80 women per 1,000 are forced to have sex by their husbands. These studies produce the same remarkable findings: One of the most common forms of sexual victimization is for a husband to force his wife into having sex or engaging in a sex act to which she objects. Russell found that twice as many women in her sample had been raped by their husbands as by strangers. Even these statistics are low, because many women do not see forced sex with a husband as rape.

Marital rape does not occur in isolation—it tends to occur along with other acts of marital violence. Researchers consistently report that women who experience marital rape are also victims of physical violence. Angela Browne (1987) found that sexual assault occurred as part of the most severe physically violent attacks.

Psychological Abuse

As with child maltreatment, there have been few attempts to assess the extent of psychological abuse among adult intimate partners. One key constraint to obtaining a measure of the extent of psychological abuse is developing an adequate definition of psychological maltreatment. Straus and Sweet (1992) using the Psychological Aggression scale from the Conflict Tactics Scales found that 74% of the men and 75% of the women surveyed for the Second National Family Violence Survey reported using at least one form of psychological aggression at least once in the previous year.

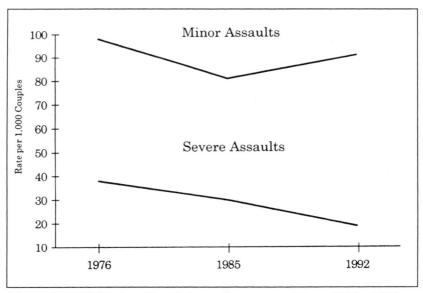

Figure 4.1. Husband-to-Wife Violence: Comparison of Rates, 1976 to 1992

Is Marital Violence Increasing?

Just as many people believe that child abuse is increasing, so too people believe that violence between partners has increased. Comparisons of the data from the First and Second National Family Violence Surveys and a 1992 national survey of alcohol and family violence (Straus & Gelles, 1986; Straus & Kaufman Kantor, 1992) found that minor assaults by husbands against wives decreased between 1976 and 1985 and then increased between 1985 and 1992 (see Figure 4.1). Severe assault by husbands, or wife beating, decreased from 38 per 1,000 in 1976 to 19 per 1,000 in 1992, a 48% decline. During the same period, there has been an 18% decline is the rate of homicides by husbands (U.S. Department of Justice, 1994b).

The rate of overall and abusive violence toward husbands remained essentially unchanged between 1976 and 1992. (The rate of minor violence was about 78 per 1,000 men in 1976 and about 93 per 1,000 men in 1992; the rate of abusive violence was about 48 per 1,000 men in 1976 and 46 per 1,000 men in 1992.)

As with their analysis of changing rates of violence toward children, the researchers (Straus & Gelles, 1986; Straus & Kaufman Kantor, 1992) attribute the decline in violence toward women to changing attitudes about wife abuse, the changing character and structure of the American family, the improving economy, increased publicity about wife abuse, and the rapid expansion of treatment and prevention programs for battered women. Whereas there were but a handful of shelters for battered women in 1976, when the First National Family Violence Survey was conducted, there were more than 1,200 shelters in 1995. Other treatment programs have been developed, including counseling groups for violent men. There has also been a growth of paid employment for married women, and working women have narrowed the gap between their wages and men's wages.

The lack of a change in the rate of violence toward men is possibly a result of the lack of attention and lack of programs for male victims of intimate violence. We will have more to say about this in the final section of this chapter.

Factors Associated With Partner Abuse

The earliest publications on the subject of wife abuse took a distinctively psychiatric view of both offender and victim. Abused women were believed to suffer from psychological disorders, as did the men who abused them. Research conducted since the 1970s finds this view of wife battery inaccurate and too simplistic. There are a number of individual, demographic, relational, and situational factors related to violence toward wives. These factors are interrelated. For example, certain relationship patterns are probably more common in certain social classes than others.

Individual Factors

Batterers. Men who assault and batter their wives have been found to have low self-esteem and vulnerable self-concepts (Neidig, Friedman, & Collins, 1986; Pagelow, 1984). A remark, insult, or comment that might not affect someone else may be interpreted as a slight, insult, or challenge to many of these men. Abusive men have also been described as feeling helpless, powerless, and inadequate (Ball, 1977; Weitzman & Dreen, 1982). Wife beaters also have been described as sadistic, passive-aggressive, addiction prone, pathologically jealous, pathologically passive, and dependent (Margolin, Sibner, & Gleberman, 1988). Gerald Hotaling and David Sugarman (1986) concluded that the picture of an assaultive man that has emerged in the literature is consistent with the diagnoses of borderline and antisocial personality disorders. Violence is frequently used as a means of trying to demonstrate power and control (Dutton & Golant, 1995). Although men use battering to control their partners, it is important to point out that all batterers are not alike. Donald Dutton (Dutton & Golant, 1995) describes three types of batterers:

- *Psychopathic wife assaulters* beat their wives and show no moral conscience, and they are cool and controlled when beating their wives. Neil Jacobson (1993) labels such men "vagal reactors." Vagal reactors showed a decline in heart rate when observed during the course of nonphysically violent arguments; in other words, they become internally calm despite being emotionally aggressive.

- *Overcontrolled wife assaulters* are distanced from their feelings and tend toward avoidance and passive-aggressive behaviors.

- *Cyclical/emotionally volatile wife abusers* demonstrate an inability to describe their feelings and an extreme need to control intimacy. Such men are involved in a cycle of moods that ebb and flow.

Edward Gondolf and Ellen Fisher (1988) also reject the notion of a monolithic characterization of batterers as sadistic psychopaths. Gondolf and Fisher analyzed data on batterers as reported by women who were victims of battering. Their statistical analysis revealed four types of batterers:

- *The sociopathic batterer* is extremely abusive toward his wife and children and is sexually abusive as well. This batterer uses severe violence outside of the home too.

- *The antisocial batterer* is also extremely abusive physically but is less injurious than the sociopathic batterer and is less likely to be violent outside of the home.

- *The chronic batterer*, although using severe verbal and physical violence, is less injurious than the previous two types of batterers and is much less likely to use weapons.

- *The sporadic batterer* uses violence less frequently than the other three types and for him, verbal and sexual violence is the least severe. He is least likely to use violence outside of the home and is apologetic after he is violent. He is the least likely to have an alcohol problem compared to the other three types of abusers.

Abused women. Psychological portraits of battered wives are difficult to interpret. One never really knows whether the personality factors described were present before the women were battered or are the result of the victimization. As with other studies of family violence, personality studies of battered women frequently use small samples, clinical samples, and often fail to have comparison groups. Thus, generalizing from these studies is difficult, and demonstrating that battered women are actually different from nonvictimized women is nearly impossible using these data.

Battered women have been described as dependent, with low self-esteem and feelings of inadequacy and helplessness (Ball, 1977; Hilberman & Munson, 1977; Shainess, 1977; Walker, 1979). Descriptive and clinical accounts consistently report a high incidence of depression and anxiety among samples of battered women (Hilberman, 1980). Barbara Star and her colleagues' (Star, Clark, Goetz, & O'Malia, 1979) review of the battered wife literature concludes that the literature is "replete with reports of low self-esteem, depressive illnesses, suicide attempts, and characterological problems among samples of battered wives" (pp. 479-480).

Hotaling and Sugarman (1990) reviewed 52 case control studies and found that only 1 of 42 risk markers for women—witnessing parental violence as a child or adolescent—was consistently related to being a victim of domestic violence.

It is best to be wary of psychological profiles of battered women. In addition to small samples and no comparison groups, samples of battered women are frequently drawn only from battered woman shelters. Thus, the researchers are studying only one type of battered woman, one who seeks help, and it is certainly unrealistic to generalize from these women to all battered women.

Second, it is likely that many of the personality factors found among samples of battered women are a consequence of being battered (Gelles & Harrop, 1991).

Alcohol. Studies of marital violence typically find a relationship between alcohol use and abuse and domestic violence. Various studies note that between 36% and 52% of wife batterers also abuse alcohol (Brekke & Saunders, 1982). Virtually every study of wife abuse conducted notes the close link between alcohol and violence (Leonard & Jacob, 1988). However, as we noted in Chapter 1, some research studies find that although there is a strong relationship between alcohol and violence, physical violence in families actually declined when drunkenness occurred "almost always" (Coleman & Straus, 1983). Also, alcohol is not an immediate antecedent of violence in the majority of families in which violence occurs (Kaufman Kantor & Straus, 1987).

That alcohol is related to wife abuse is clear. What is not clear is how alcohol is related to violence. Do men drink, lose control, and then abuse? Or does alcohol become a convenient excuse or rationalization for violent behavior? Cross-cultural studies of alcohol use and studies of marital violence suggest that alcohol itself does not lead to violence; rather, men drink (or say they drink) to have a socially acceptable excuse for violent behavior (Fagan, 1990; Gelles, 1974, 1993).

Demographic Factors

Results of the National Family Violence Survey indicate that all forms of marital violence occur most frequently among those under 30 years of age (Gelles, Wolfner, & Lackner, 1994; Straus et al., 1980). The rate of marital violence among those under 30 years of age is more than double the rate for next older age group (ages 31 to 50). The rate of domestic violence peaks when offenders are age 24 (Steffensmeier, Allan, Harer, & Streifel, 1989).

Studies that examine women who seek help from agencies or shelters also find that the mean age is 30 or younger (Fagan, Stewart, & Stewart, 1983; Gayford, 1975).

The relationship between race, ethnicity, and domestic violence is inconsistent. Data from the National Family Violence Surveys found that wife abuse was more common in Black households than white households and more common among Latinos than whites (Hampton & Gelles, 1994; Straus & Smith, 1990). On the other hand, data from the NCVS (Bachman, 1994) indicate that the rate of intimate adult violence is essentially unrelated to race: The rate for Blacks was 5.8 per 1,000; for whites, 5.4 per 1,000; and for Latinos, 5.5 per 1,000.

Obviously, if there is a relationship between race and domestic violence, race is not the only factor in play. Income and occupational status are probably also associated with the slightly increased rates of wife abuse among Blacks and Latinos.

Marital violence can occur at any stage of a marriage, but as the data on age would appear to indicate, newer marriages have the highest risk of wife abuse. Maria Roy (1977) found that the highest percentage of battered women were married from 2.5 to 5 years. Another study reported that the median length of a violent marriage was 5 years (Fagan et al., 1983).

The most severe violence tends to occur immediately after the breakup of an intimate relationship. Women are more likely to be victims of a homicide when they are estranged from their husbands. The risk of a homicide is greatest in the first 2 months after a separation (Wilson & Daly, 1993).

Economic Factors

Irrespective of the method, sample, or research design, studies of marital violence support the hypothesis that spousal violence is more likely to occur in low-income, low-socioeconomic-status families. These findings do not mean that wife abuse is confined only to low-income, low-status families. One woman who was married to a Fortune 500 corporate executive described how her husband beat her and how, to escape his violence, she slept in their Continental Mark IV every Saturday night. A good deal of violence in middle- and upper-class families is kept secret. Neighbors do not live close by and do not call the police. Upper-class husbands seem to have more success in keeping the police from arresting them. Nevertheless, it would appear that the probability of wife abuse occurring in high-income, upper-class homes is less than the probability of occurrence among the poor.

One of the main factors associated with wife battery is the employment status of the husband. Being unemployed is devastating to men in our society. It is a clear demonstration that they are not fulfilling society's expectation that men are the family providers. Unemployed men have rates of wife assault that are almost double the rates for employed men (Gayford, 1975; Prescott & Letko, 1977; Rounsaville, 1978). Men who are employed part-time have even higher rates, probably because they

have the worst of all possible worlds—no full-time job and not eligible
for unemployment or other benefits (Straus et al., 1980).

Experience With and Exposure to Violence

As with child battering, wife battering is related to experiences with
violence. Individuals who have experienced violent childhoods are more
likely to grow up and assault their wives than men who have not
experienced childhood violence (Browne, 1987; Fagan et al., 1983;
Gelles, 1974; Hotaling & Sugarman, 1986; Pagelow, 1984). Studies also
find that observing parental violence is related to spousal aggression
(Browne, 1987; Pagelow, 1981; Rosenbaum & O'Leary, 1981). This
finding is consistent for men—those who observe their parents use
violence are much more likely to grow up to be abusive partners. The
evidence for women is inconsistent, and it is not clear whether women
who observe their parents' violence are likely to become violent adults
(O'Leary, 1988).

Again, it is very important to introduce the caution that a violent
background does not predetermine a violent adulthood. Although the
chances of being an offender and victim are increased if one grows up in
a violent home, there are many violent people who had limited exposure
to violence as children, and some people who experienced extremely
violent childhoods grow up to be nonviolent.

Relationship Factors

One of the most compelling indicators that domestic violence is not
purely a product of individual pathology is the finding that certain
properties of marital relations raise the likelihood of violence. That the
structural properties of marriage and family life are involved means that
abuse cannot be solely attributed to "bad" or "sick" people.

Early studies of domestic violence found that men whose educational
attainment and occupational status were lower than their wives were more
likely to assault their wives than men who were better educated and had
better jobs than their spouses (Gelles, 1974; O'Brien, 1971). Additional
research bears out the hypothesis that status inconsistency and status
incompatibility are related to marital violence. One example of status
inconsistency is where a husband's educational background is considerably higher than his occupational attainment (e.g., a Ph.D. who drives a

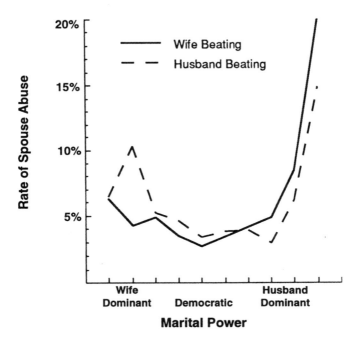

Figure 4.2. Marital Violence by Marital Power
SOURCE: Gelles and Straus (1988).

taxi cab). Status incompatibility is when the husband, whom society expects to be the head of the family, has less education and a poorer job than his wife. In both of these cases, the risk of marital violence is elevated (Hornung, McCullough, & Sugimoto, 1981; Rounsaville, 1978; Steinmetz, 1978b).

Decision-making patterns or power balance was also found to be related to domestic violence. Democratic households—homes where the decision making is shared—are the least violent families (see Figure 4.2). Homes where all the decisions are made either by the wife or the husband have the highest rates of violence.

A final relationship factor is that if there is one type of family violence in a home, there is a good chance that another form of violence will be present. Child abuse rates are higher in homes where there is spouse abuse (Fagan & Browne, 1994; Finkelhor, 1983; Gelles & Straus, 1988; Hilberman & Munson, 1977; Straus et al., 1980).

Stress and Isolation

Social stress and social isolation are two final factors that are strongly related to the risk of wife abuse. Unemployment, financial problems, sexual difficulties, low job satisfaction, large family size, and poor housing conditions are all related to marital violence. The more socially isolated a family is, the higher the risk that there will be wife abuse (Fagan & Browne, 1994).

Staying in or Leaving Battering Relationships

One thing is quite clear from the review of research of wife abuse—domestic violence is not a one-time event. Rather, it is a pattern that endures over a considerable period of time. Because domestic violence is a recurrent behavior, and because the victims—women—are adults and not helpless children, some people have assumed that the solution to marital violence is for the battered women to leave or divorce their husbands. We noted in Chapter 1 that one of the most pervasive myths in the field of intimate violence is the myth that battered wives like being hit, otherwise they would leave. Considerable research has been conducted that refutes the myth of the masochistic battered wife. In general, the studies find that many factors—economic, relational, cultural, and social—constrain women from leaving a battering relationship.

The psychologist Lenore Walker (1979) examined numerous cases of battered women and developed the theory of "learned helplessness" to explain why so many women endure such extreme violence for so long. Walker noted that women who experience repeated physical assaults at the hands of their husbands have much lower self-concepts than women whose marriages were free from violence. Walker postulated that the repeated beatings and lower self-concepts leave women with the feeling that they cannot control what will happen to them. They feel they are unable to protect themselves from further assaults and feel incapable of controlling the events that go on around them. Thus, like laboratory animals who have experienced repeated shocks from which there is no apparent escape, battered women eventually learn that they are helpless to prevent violent attacks.

Learned helplessness implies a rather passive nature of battered women, and it is important not to confuse the situation of women who are battered with the situation of the laboratory animals from whom the theory of learned helplessness was derived. Walker (1993) has revised her initial conceptualization of learned helplessness and proposes that women in battering relationships experience a constellation of effects that make up the battered woman syndrome (BWS). The BWS is a pattern of psychological symptoms called post-traumatic stress disorder (PTSD). Criteria of PTSD include (a) experiencing a stressor (such as battering) that can cause a traumatic response; (b) psychological symptoms lasting more than a month; (c) measurable cognitive and memory changes; (d) at least three measurable avoidance symptoms; and (e) at least two measurable arousal symptoms, such as hypervigilance or an exaggerated startle response. Walker argues that the psychological trauma caused by repeated battering explains some women's reluctance to flee a battering relationship or other women's decisions to kill abusive husbands.

Most battered women are far from passive. They call the police, they go to social workers or mental health agencies, they flee to shelters or the homes of friends or parents, and they fight back. But in many ways, women are constrained by social forces from permanently leaving a violent relationship. Legal writer Elizabeth Truninger (1971) lists seven factors that help explain why women do not break off relationships with abusive men: (a) the women have negative self-concepts; (b) they believe men will reform; (c) economic hardship; (d) they have children who need a father's economic support; (e) they doubt they can get along alone; (f) they believe divorcees are stigmatized; and (g) it is difficult for women with children to get work.

Lee Bowker (1993) explains that women's reactions to experiencing domestic violence and their decisions about whether to stay or leave a violent relationship are not the products of the personalities of battered women but rather are the result of the many social, psychological, economic, and physical factors that hold women in abusive relationships. Although many battered women do not leave their abusers, and many who leave return again, battered women do resist their husbands and use a variety of strategies to protect themselves and their children.

In my own research, I compared battered women who stayed with their violent husbands to women who called the police, sought a divorce, or went to a mental health agency for help. I found that certain factors distinguished women who stayed in the violent relationship from women who sought help or left a violent husband. First, those women who leave seem to experience the most severe and frequent violence. Second, women who experienced more violence as children were more likely to remain in violent relationships. In addition, women with limited educational attainment and occupational skills were more likely to stay with battering husbands. The fewer resources a woman had, the less power she had, the more she was entrapped in a marriage and the more she suffered at the hands of her husband (Gelles, 1976).

The sociologist Mildred Pagelow (1981) investigated the situation of battered women. Her research on women who sought help from shelters confirms some of my findings, whereas other findings are not supported in Pagelow's study. Pagelow administered questionnaires to 350 women who had sought temporary residence for themselves or their children in battered woman shelters. Severity and frequency of violence did not influence the decision of whether to leave. Whereas some of the women in the shelters endured years of violence and abuse, others fled after the first or second incident. Also, Pagelow did not find support for the association between violence experienced as a child and the decision to stay or leave. Actually, shelter residents who experienced childhood violence were more apt to leave after the first incident of violence or else they remained in a violent home a shorter time than other women. Pagelow did find that the resources women had (education, occupation, income) did influence whether they stayed or left a violent husband.

The sociologists Michael Strube and Linda Barbour (1983) talked with 98 battered wives and also confirmed that economically dependent women were more likely to remain with an abusive husband. They also found that wives who stayed with violent men reported they were more "committed" to the marital relationship.

Instead of categorizing battered women as experiencing learned helplessness, Edward Gondolf and Ellen Fisher (1988) see battered women as "active survivors." Gondolf and Fisher's research found that women respond to abuse with helpseeking efforts that are largely unmet. Abused women often seek help from community services that are overwhelmed and limited in their resources and therefore do not try as hard as they might to help the abused women. Gondolf and Fisher studied women who sought services from shelters for battered women in Texas. The main outcome factors that Gondolf and Fisher examined were the women's planned living arrangements on leaving the shelter, the women's actual living arrangements, and the reported level of violence after a follow-up period. In terms of women's plans to return to live with their batterers after leaving the shelter, one of the main factors that influenced this decision was whether the batterer was involved with a counseling program. Nineteen percent of the women without batterers in counseling planned to return to their batterers, whereas 53% of women with batterers in counseling said they would return to live with the batterer. Apparently, when a woman's batterer is enrolled in a counseling program, the woman is more likely to believe (or want to believe) that "this time he *is* really going to change." Obviously, this belief allows batterers to use counseling as another form of manipulation of their partners. A second factor that influenced whether women would return to the batterer was the women's level of economic independence.

Ola Barnett and Alyce LaViolette (1993) criticize the concept of learned helplessness. They place the issue of why battered women stay into a larger cultural context. They explain that the socialization of girls to women both within the family and the larger culture involves the learning of a belief system that devalues women, especially unmarried women, and creates a sense of female responsibility for the maintenance of an emotionally stable family. Thus, the failure of a relationship or marriage, even as a result of severe violence and abuse, is assumed to be the fault of the woman. Battered women learn to endure abuse and remain in unhealthy relationships. Barnett and LaViolette refer to this learning process as "learned hopefulness." Learned hopefulness is a battered woman's ongoing belief that her partner will change his abusive behavior or that he will change his personality. Learned hopefulness explains why the women Gondolf and Fisher studied were more likely to return to their abusive partners if the men were enrolled in counseling programs for batterers.

In addition to learned hopefulness and economic dependence, fear plays a role in women's decision to stay or leave violent relationships. Battered women may fear retaliation if they leave or try to leave a violent relationship. They also may fear losing their children. Many battered women report that their partners threaten to kidnap or even kill their children if the women try to leave the relationship. The data cited earlier about the higher rate of violence and homicide when women leave relationships reinforce the fear battered women feel about leaving.

Stopping the Violence

Although the stereotype of batterers is that they begin by using infrequent and less serious forms of violence and eventually escalate to frequent and severe violence, it is apparent that although some men do escalate their use of violence, other men appear to stop physical violence for some period of time. Scott Feld and Murray Straus (1989) followed up a subsample of violent men who were surveyed in the 1985 National Family Violence Survey. More than 800 of the married respondents who reported one or more assaults in their marriage were followed up a year later. In addition, a subsample of nonviolent respondents were contacted a year later. Thirty-three percent of the most violent perpetrators did not assault their wives a year later, and an additional 10% hit their wives but did not use the serious form of violence they had used the year before. Of course, 57% of the severely violent men were still using severe forms of violence a year later. Ten percent of the men who were not violent in the first year of the study were reported as using minor (7%) or severe (3%) violence in the second year.

Although it is certainly possible that some of the reported desistance may be the result of inaccurate reporting by the respondents, and although some men who desisted in acts of physical violence may have escalated their use of psychological or emotional violence, it is also probable that a portion of violent men do stop using violence, at least for some period of time.

Desistance may be the result of a man being arrested and jailed, may be the result of enrolling and completing a counseling program for batterers, or may be due to other factors. The sociologist Lee Bowker (1983) examined the stories and situations of women who chose to stay with their husbands and whose husbands stopped their violent behavior. Bowker conducted 136 in-depth interviews over a 9-month period with women who stayed with their husbands and whose husbands stopped using violence. Bowker used a variety of strategies to locate these women—referrals from social service agencies, radio and television appearances by members of the research team, newspaper advertisements, and so on.

Bowker (1983) learned that the techniques used by women to try to get their husbands to stop using violence clustered into three types: (a) personal strategies, including talking, promising, threatening, hiding, passive defense, aggressive defense, and avoidance; (b) use of informal help sources, including family members, in-laws, neighbors, friends, and shelters; and (c) formal help sources, including the police, social service agencies, and lawyers and district attorneys. The most common personal strategy was passive defense—covering one's body with arms, hands, or feet. The most common informal strategy was friends; social services were the leading formal source of help.

Which technique worked best? There was no simple answer. Bowker reported that no single strategy is guaranteed to stop violence, but almost any strategy or help-source can ultimately work. What mattered was "the woman's showing her determination that the violence must stop now" (Bowker, 1983, p. 131). Of course, the decision and responsibility to actually stop is the man's, but without the woman's determination, his stopping is much less likely.

Murray Straus and I used the opportunity of our Second National Family Violence Survey to extend the research carried out by Lee Bowker. Whereas Bowker advertised for a small sample of women in Milwaukee, Straus and I had access to more than 3,000 women representative of the entire population of married women, women living with men, or women recently divorced in the United States (Gelles & Straus, 1988). We asked what the immediate reaction was to being hit. Crying was the immediate response that was most frequently reported. Shock, surprise, and the stunning realization that a woman has been hit by someone she loves probably explains this. Many women reacted more actively. The second most common immediate response was yelling and cursing at a violent spouse. Nearly one in four victims (24%) hit their attacker back—despite the obvious risks of escalating the violence. Not surprisingly, those women who were victims of severe violence were somewhat more reluctant to hit their husbands back than were victims of minor violence. Immediately seeking help from the police was the least likely response, especially for victims of minor violence. Less than 3% of the victims of minor violence immediately called the police after they were attacked, whereas 5 times that percentage (14%) of the victims of beatings, choking, and other forms of severe violence immediately called the police.

After we talked with victims of intimate violence about their immediate reactions to being hit, we turned our attention to the more deliberate and long-term steps taken by assaulted women to get their husbands or partners to stop hurting or threatening them. The single most common strategy that victims used to attempt to prevent future violence was avoiding their spouses and staying away from certain topics of conversation. The second most common long-range prevention strategy was trying to talk husbands out of being violent. The women who use the talking strategy generally try to use logic and rational discussion and argument to persuade husbands to stop being violent. We found that the third most widely used mechanism for attempting to limit violence was hiding or leaving. In just the past year before we interviewed them, nearly all of the battered wives (7 out of 10) had left their assaultive spouses. Keeping in mind that these are women who have been battered for a number of years, it is reasonable to assume that every one of them left for some period of time during the course of the battering.

We also asked women to assess the effectiveness of the strategies they used. Just as Bowker discovered, the most effective strategy for stopping wife beating was a woman's conviction and determination that the violence must stop now. The single most effective strategy employed by the national sample of women was persuading husbands to promise not to be violent again. The least effective strategy was hitting back.

A Note on Men as Victims

The results of the Second National Family Violence Survey (summarized in Table 4.1) included data on violence toward husbands. Of the wives surveyed, 4.4% reported that they had engaged in violence toward their husbands that could be considered abusive (Gelles & Straus, 1988). Violence toward men, or husband abuse, has been a controversial area in the study of domestic violence. There has been considerable rhetoric on this topic but, unfortunately, precious little scientific data.

In 1978, the sociologist Suzanne Steinmetz (1978a) published an article designed to demonstrate that husbands as well as wives were the

victims of violence in the home. Steinmetz reviewed numerous investigations of family violence and found, contrary to some feminist and
scholarly claims, that women were not the only victims of spousal
violence. Steinmetz went on to claim that it was husband and not wife
abuse that was the most underreported form of family violence. Steinmetz
was immediately challenged and attacked by feminists and scholars alike
for misreading, misinterpreting, and misrepresenting her findings (see
Pleck, Pleck, Grossman, & Bart, 1978).

Unlike most debates among scholars, this one spilled over into the
public media (*Time*, "The Today Show," "Donahue,") and even into the
syndicated column of Ann Landers (for a detailed discussion of the public
debate, see Jones, 1980). Sadly, the debate boiled in the public domain,
but the issue received little attention in the scholarly arena. The issue of
so-called battered husbands heated up again in 1994, in the wake of the
killing of Nicole Brown Simpson and Ronald Goldman and the attendant
publicity to the issue of violence against women. Some researchers and
newspaper columnists cited the data on battered men to counter the claims
that there was a "war against women" in the United States. Those who
claim that there are many battered men frequently cite our 1985 National
Family Violence Survey data and claim that the data reveal that there are
as many (or more) battered men as there are battered women. In addition,
writers often note that our data revealed that women use as serious forms
of violence as do men and initiate the violence about as often as men do.[2]
Unfortunately, almost all of those who try to make the case that there are
as many battered men as battered women tend to omit or reduce to a
parenthetical phrase the fact that no matter how much violence there is or
who initiates the violence, women are as much as 10 times more likely
than men to be injured in acts of domestic violence.

It is quite clear that men are struck by their wives. It is also clear that
because men are typically larger than their wives and usually have more
social resources at their command, that they do not have as much physical
or social damage inflicted on them as is inflicted on women. Data from
studies of households where the police intervened in domestic violence
clearly indicate that men are rarely the victims of battery (Berk, Berk,
Loseke, & Rauma, 1983). Thus, although the data in Table 4.1 show
similar rates of hitting, when injury is considered, marital violence is
primarily a problem of victimized women.

Notes

1. Although this estimate of the prevalence of sexual violence in dating relationships is widely cited, a number of questions have been raised about the methodological rigor of the research on dating and acquaintance rape. Neil Gilbert (1993) has raised questions about the ambiguity of the questions used to measure date and acquaintance rape and the inconsistencies in the reported findings. Gilbert, although acknowledging that date and acquaintance rape is an important social concern, argues that the estimates of the extent of date and acquaintance rape greatly inflate the actual extent of this social problem.

2. For examples of articles and columns pointing out the existence of battered men, see Judith Sherven and James Sniechowski (1994), Warren Farrell (1994), John Leo (1994), and Armin Brott (1994).

DISCUSSION QUESTIONS

1. Compare the nature of courtship violence to the nature of violence within marriage. Is the marriage license a hitting license, or are there other factors that increase the risk that intimates will be violent toward one another?

2. Discuss the various ways economic factors influence the chances that spouse abuse will occur.

3. Why is it unfair to blame battered women for remaining with their battering spouses? What resources or facilities in the community could help women who wanted to leave their violent husbands?

4. Are there battered husbands?

SUGGESTED ASSIGNMENTS

1. Identify the services that exist for battered women in your community (e.g., shelters or safe houses, hot lines, counseling groups for battered women).

2. Talk to someone who works in a shelter or a safe house. Is the address of the shelter public or a secret? How many women and children can the shelter hold? Does the shelter ever turn away women? Why? What is the philosophy of the shelter—how do the workers approach the problem of violence toward women?

3. Create a resource book for victims of spouse abuse in your community —include the names, addresses, and telephone numbers of all resources that could be used by victims of spouse abuse.

4. Find out what services (if any) are available for victims of courtship violence at your college or university.

5

HIDDEN VICTIMS

Siblings, Adolescents, Parents, Elders, and Gay and Lesbian Couples

The public and professional attention paid to child abuse and violence against women has had the unanticipated consequence of leading many people to believe that women and children are the most vulnerable and most frequent victims of intimate violence. Yet children and women are not the most vulnerable victims of intimate violence, nor are they the most commonly victimized family members—siblings are.

This chapter examines violent intimate relationships that have largely been overlooked by the public, researchers, and members of the social service and public policy communities. Each form of violence has been overlooked for a slightly different reason. Violence between siblings is so common that people rarely think of these events as family violence. I have already mentioned adolescent victims of family violence when I discussed violence toward children (see Chapter 3). Discussions of child abuse rarely extend beyond the youngest victims. Older victims of parental violence tend to be blamed for their own victimization. Teenagers are thought of as causing their own victimization, and as we blame the victim, we tend to overlook this violent family relationship. Parent abuse is considered almost humorous by those who first hear of it. The large majority of parent victims are so shamed by their victimization that they are reluctant to discuss anything but the most severe incidents, and when they do report, they, like adolescent victims, are blamed for being hit. Elders are also victims of intimate violence at the hands of their partners, children, and caretakers. They may be the most hidden victims, because one of the aspects of aging in our society is the departure of elders from their regular and normal systems and institutions of social interaction (e.g., work). Finally, violence among gay and lesbian couples has been almost completely been ignored by researchers and practitioners.

Although research on most of these forms of intimate violence is scarce (there has been an increase in research on elder abuse in the past few years), any book on family violence would be incomplete without a discussion of violent relations other than parent to child and between husband and wife.

Sibling Violence

Normative Attitudes Toward Sibling Violence

Sibling violence is the most common form of intimate violence. Siblings hitting one another is so common that few people consider these behaviors violent. The existence of social norms that encourage expressions of aggressive behavior among siblings hinders the recognition of sibling violence as abnormal and worthy of serious concern. Most parents view conflict among siblings as an inevitable part of growing up. However, as the sociologist Suzanne Steinmetz (1977) notes, our complacency about sibling violence needs to be reexamined in light of statistics that indicate that in Philadelphia between 1948 and 1952 and in New York in 1965, 3% of all homicides were sibling homicides (Bard, 1971; Wolfgang, 1958). More recent statistics on family homicides reveal that 1.5% of all murder victims are killed by siblings. This constitutes about 10% of all murders in families (Dawson & Langan, 1994).

Sociologists who have studied violence between siblings have found that parents often feel it is important for their children to learn how to handle themselves in violent situations. Many parents do not actively discourage their children from becoming involved in disputes with their siblings. In fact, parents may try to ignore aggressive interactions and only become involved when minor situations are perceived as escalating into major confrontations. Sibling rivalry is considered a "normal" part of relations between siblings, and many parents believe that such rivalry provides a good training ground for the successful management of aggressive behavior in the real world. American parents generally feel that some exposure to aggression is a positive experience that should occur early in life, although over the years support for exposure to aggression has declined. Whereas in the late 1960s, 7 out of 10 Americans agreed with the statement: "When a boy is growing up it is important for him to have a few fist fights" (Stark & McEvoy, 1970), by 1995 only 1 in 5 of those surveyed agreed with this statement (Gallup Organization, 1995).

Steinmetz (1977) was one of the first social scientists to examine violence between siblings. In her study of sibling conflict in a representative sample of 57 intact families in Delaware, she found that it was sometimes difficult to get parents to discuss sibling violence, not because they were ashamed or embarrassed to admit such behavior, but because the parents often did not view their children's actions as abusive and worthy of mentioning. When questioned further about particular incidents, parents said that they found their children's conduct annoying but they did not perceive the situation as one of conflict. When prompted, most parents will freely discuss or admit to the existence of sibling violence in their homes. Parents willingly tell friends, neighbors, and researchers, without embarrassment or restraint, how their children are constantly involved in argumentative and abusive behavior toward one another. When Steinmetz asked the parents in her study: "How do your children get along?" she received such statements as

Terrible! They fight all the time.

Oh, it's just constant, but I understand that this is normal.

I talk to other people and their children are the same way. (Steinmetz, 1977, p. 43)

From these typical comments, it becomes obvious that parents view such frequent and violent confrontations as inevitable.

Perhaps parents may be somewhat justified in their assessment of the inevitability of sibling violence. The existence of sibling rivalry has been documented throughout history beginning with the biblical story of Cain and Abel, in which Cain kills his brother. This is perhaps the earliest, although certainly not the only, recorded account of sibling violence. Evidence of violence among siblings can also be found in more contemporary sources. However, what is lacking in the recorded accounts of sibling violence is information from controlled, scientific research projects. In the early 1970s, Suzanne Steinmetz and Murray Straus reported that prior to their own investigations into the causes, frequency, and patterns of sibling violence, information on noninfant, nonfatal sibling violence was almost nonexistent. This situation persists in the 1990s.

Those research articles that appear in the scientific literature deal almost exclusively with sibling murders (Adelson, 1972; Bender, 1959; Sargent, 1962; Smith, 1965). Society appears only to take notice of the most extreme expressions of sibling violence. Levels of violence among siblings that do not exceed the levels defined as socially acceptable or normal still go unnoticed by both researchers and society in general (Pagelow, 1989). This historic acceptance of sibling violence as normal and inevitable has made it difficult to establish if the rates of sibling violence have increased, decreased, or remained the same. Trend data simply do not exist. Even today, there are relatively few studies on sibling violence, and the level of awareness concerning sibling violence as a significant form of family violence is low.

Extent of Violence Between Siblings

Steinmetz's (1977) previously mentioned investigation into sibling rivalry discovered frequent occurrences of sibling conflict in American families. The parents in 49 families recorded the frequency and types of violent behavior occurring between their offspring during a 1-week period. Steinmetz reported that a total of 131 sibling conflicts occurred during this period, ranging from short-lived arguments to more serious confrontations. She believes, however, that this figure, although high, was probably a considerable underestimation of the true extent of sibling aggression. She noted that there are many problems inherent in relying on parents to record the frequency of sibling conflicts. For example, in most of the families in Steinmetz's sample both parents worked, reducing the amount of time the parents actually spent with their children. This in turn reduced the opportunity of parents to observe and record violent behaviors between children. Steinmetz also found that parents often would record a series of events as one incident because the events were all related to the same causal event. The way in which parents chose to record conflicts eventually affected the total number of conflicts observed. Finally, parents were at times too busy to record their children's behavior. Recording the violent incidents at a later time increased the probability that some occurrences of sibling conflict could have been forgotten. Regardless of the shortcomings in the recording technique, Steinmetz demonstrated that sibling violence occurred and the frequency of occurrences appeared to be quite high. In subsequent studies, Steinmetz (1982) found that between 63% and 68% of adolescent siblings in the families she studied used physical violence to resolve conflicts with brothers and sisters.

Several years later, a team of sociologists (Straus et al., 1980) conducted a nationally representative study on family violence. Sibling violence was one of several forms of family violence investigated. They reported the startling statistic that slightly more than four out of five (82%) children between the ages of 3 and 17, residing in the United States and having one or more siblings living at home, engaged in at least one violent act toward a sibling during a 1-year period. This translated into approximately 36.3 million children being violent toward a sibling within a year's time. Much of the violence that siblings engage in includes pushing, slapping, shoving, and throwing things. Some people have argued that these behaviors are not really serious and serve to overestimate the real rates of sibling violence. Therefore, when these "lesser" forms of violence are excluded and the researchers examined only the more severe forms of violence (such as kicking, biting, pushing, hitting with an object, and beating up), the rates were still alarmingly high. Straus and his colleagues estimate that over 19 million children a year engage in acts of abusive violence against a sibling.

There have been only a few other studies that report on the extent of violence between siblings, and most of these studies are based on nonrepresentative clinical samples. Ginny NiCarthy (1983) reported that 40% to 50% of the female teenagers she worked with had been assaulted by brothers. Megan Goodwin and Bruce Roscoe (1990) surveyed 272 high school juniors and seniors and found that 65% of the females and 64% of the males indicated they had perpetrated some form of sibling violence; 64% of the females and 66% of the males reported they were victims of sibling violence. The less dangerous forms of violence were the most common, but 3.4% of those surveyed reported being threatened with a knife or gun and 2.6% reported threatening a sibling with a weapon. The National Crime Victimization Survey includes data on victim-offender relationship, but these data tend to underreport sibling violence, first, because the survey is limited to individuals 12 years of age or older, and second, because respondents are asked to report on crime victimization. As I noted earlier, violence at the hands of a brother or sister is rarely viewed as criminal behavior. Only 1.3% of women who reported they were the victims of a violent crime and 0.3% of male victims of a violent crime reported that the offender was a sibling (Bachman, 1994).

Sibling sexual abuse is also common and overlooked. Here again, there is a reluctance to view sibling sexual abuse as deviant. David Finkelhor (1979) found that of the 796 undergraduate college students he surveyed, 15% of the women and 10% of the men reported some type of sexual experience involving a sibling. Based on this, Finkelhor speculated that sibling sexual abuse may be the most prevalent form of sexual abuse and incest, but his respondents were equally split in terms of viewing such sexual experiences positively or negatively. Females who reported sexual victimization at the hands of siblings were more likely to view the experiences negatively, largely because of the physical coercion that was part of the sexual experience. The actual extent of sibling sexual abuse depends on the definition of what constitutes abuse. Diane Russell (1984) used a narrower definition of sexual abuse (she asked whether respondents had experienced "at least one sexually abusive experience with a brother before the age of 18") and found that 2% of her 930 female respondents reported sexual abuse with a sibling. Clearly, some of the sexual interaction between siblings is sexual exploration or what may be called "sex play." But some sexual interaction is physically or psychologically coercive and exploitative and is abusive. A review of studies of sexual abuse based on nonclinical samples suggests that between 2% and 4% of children experience abusive sexual relationships with siblings (Haugaard, 1994). Sibling abuse, however, although less common than abuse by fathers, stepfathers, or uncles, goes on longer than abuse by other relatives (O'Brien, 1991).

Factors Related to Sibling Violence

Sex. Given that sibling violence occurs with alarming frequency, one important question is whether all children engage in these violent acts with the same frequency or if these aggressive actions are being carried out by a particular category of children. Although children of all ages and both sexes engage in violence and abuse against a brother or sister, there appears to be some difference in the rates at which they are violent. A commonly held belief in our society is that boys are more physically aggressive and girls are more verbally aggressive. One would expect, then, that sibling violence is initiated primarily by brothers. Although the research on sibling violence tends to support this commonsense belief, the support is not as overwhelming as one might expect (Straus et al., 1980). Whereas 83% of boys were aggressive toward a brother or sister, so were 74% of girls! At all ages, girls were less violent than boys, but the difference was relatively small. William Mangold and Patricia Koski (1990) surveyed college-aged students and found that males were more violent toward brothers than were females, but there was no significant difference between males and females when the object of the violence was a sister.

Age. Research into sibling violence also confirms the belief that as children grow older, the rates of using violence to resolve conflicts between siblings decrease (Steinmetz, 1977; Straus et al., 1980). This could be the result of children becoming better equipped at using verbal skills to settle disputes. Also, as children grow older, they spend less and less time in each others' company. Older children spend more time away from home and away from potential sibling conflicts.

Steinmetz (1977) found that the factors precipitating conflicts varied with age. Younger children were more likely to have conflicts centered around possessions, especially toys. One family in Steinmetz's sample reported that during a 1-week period, their young children fought over "the use of a glider, sharing a truck, sharing a tricycle, knocking down one child's building blocks and taking them." Young adolescent conflicts focused on territory, with adolescents becoming very upset if a sibling invaded their personal space. "They fuss. They say, 'He's sitting in my seat,' or 'He has got an inch of his pants on the line where I am supposed to be' " (Steinmetz, 1977, p. 53). One father, driven to the breaking point by his children constantly fighting in the back seat of the car, took a can of red paint and painted boundary lines on the back seat and floor in an attempt to end disputes over personal space. Teenage conflicts, although less in number, still exist. These conflicts centered around responsibilities, obligations, and social awareness. Teenagers were more likely to be verbally aggressive and found that hollering was usually effective in conflict situations, especially when the siblings differed in opinions.

Other factors. Little is known about the factors that may be potentially associated with sibling violence. Those who have studied sibling murder often attribute the cause of such extreme aggression to jealousy. Dr. Adelson, after examining several children who had committed murder, concluded that preschoolers are capable of homicidal rage when they are threatened regarding their sense of security in the family unit. Kay Tooley's (1977) investigation of "murderously aggressive children" suggests that younger victims of sibling violence may sometimes be family scapegoats. However, it has not yet been established if lesser forms of sibling aggression can be attributed to the same factors believed to be associated with murder.

Research on violent adolescents generally concludes that the factors associated with intimate adult violence (child abuse and spouse abuse) are of little use in helping to explain violence among children (Cornell & Gelles, 1982). In other words, children are not committing acts of violence for the same reason as adults.

Finally, some researchers have postulated that sibling violence is a learned response. Although it is commonly believed that children will resort to violence as a natural way to resolve conflicts, Straus et al. (1980) believe that siblings learn from their parents that physical punishment is an appropriate technique for resolving conflicts. Children raised in nonviolent environments learn there are a variety of nonviolent techniques available for resolving conflicts with brothers and sisters and later with their spouses and children.

Violence Toward Adolescents

Although young children are the most frequent targets of physical abuse, abuse is not limited to very young children (see Chapter 3). Preteens and teenagers are experiencing a wide range of violent treatments at the hands of their parents. Although it is true that the rates of physical violence, abuse, and homicide at the hands of one's family members decline as children grow older, researchers who have examined the rates of adolescent victimization were surprised at the number of teenagers being mistreated in American families (Finkelhor & Dziuba-Leatherman, 1994b; Wauchope & Straus, 1990).

Societal attitudes perpetuate the myth that adolescents are rarely abused by their parents. As teenagers acquire greater physical strength with age, parents may begin to fear retaliation at the hands of children whose physical strength may surpass their own. For those children who are being struck, many people believe they precipitate or deserve being hit. Common sense sometimes suggests that teenagers frustrate their parents to such an extent that they deserve what they get!

The status of adolescents in our society is much the same as that of younger children. Both are considered the property and responsibility of their parents. Parents are granted societal permission to engage in a wide range of behaviors when disciplining their offspring. Although parents are expected to practice restraint when disciplining, the use of physical punishment is sanctioned as an acceptable behavior even for teenage children. Both young children and adolescents are relegated to a subordinate position within the family structure, with parents being granted the right to bestow rewards and punishments as they see fit (Gil, 1970). Both preschoolers and teenagers are known for their difficult stages of development. Frustration in parents is often generated from young children going through the "terrible twos" stage. The terrible twos may be revisited as teenagers go through a stage of rebellion and independence. Preschool children are too young to be reasoned with, and teenagers do not wish to be reasoned with. It is this ability to generate frustration within their parents and create stress in the family unit as a whole that places young children and teenagers in the vulnerable position of being victimized. Adolescents have reached a point in their development in being able to make effective use of the verbal skills they have acquired through years of conflict resolutions with family members. The biggest complaint among parents of adolescents in Steinmetz's study on parent-child conflict was the "smart talk mouthiness" used by adolescents in both sibling and parent-child interactions. Steinmetz (1977) describes the adolescents in her sample as being "verbally aggressive" and frequently engaging in hollering, threatening, and arguing.

If the position of young children and teenagers is so similar in our society, why has society become so deeply concerned with protecting the rights of younger children while ignoring the plight of adolescents? The answer to this question can again be traced to differences in expectations parents have for their younger children versus their older children. Parents expect their adolescents to begin acting in a more mature and responsible manner as they approach adulthood. They expect adolescents to be able to follow orders and to begin internalizing their system of values. Parents do not hold the same expectations for their preschoolers. Therefore, when adolescents fail to live up to their parents' expectations of them, parents sometimes use physical force as a way of asserting their parental control. Society is more likely to condone the use of physical force directed at an adolescent due to the belief that adolescents deserve such treatment.

Adolescents are also perceived as being better able to fend for themselves in disputes with their parents. Adolescents are larger and stronger and, therefore, better able to protect themselves or avoid confrontations altogether. Although this may be true, Martha Mulligan (1977), in her sample of over 250 college students attending an eastern university, found that 8 in 100 students in her sample had been physically injured by a parent while they lived at home during their senior year of high school.

Extent of Violence Toward Adolescents

Although researchers are not in total agreement as to the exact extent of adolescent abuse, they do agree that violence toward adolescents is a legitimate and significant form of family violence that occurs more frequently than is generally assumed. In fact, researchers have been generally surprised at the rate at which parents were physically abusing their adolescent children. The national survey of officially recognized and reported child maltreatment (Burgdorf, 1980) found that 47% of recognized victims of maltreatment were between the ages of 12 and 17. Data collected by the National Center on Child Abuse and Neglect reveal that adolescents 13 to 18 years old represented about 20% of officially reported victims of maltreatment in 1993 (U.S. Department of Health and Human Services, National Center on Child Abuse and Neglect, 1995). David Finkelhor and Jennifer Dziuba-Leatherman (1994a) surveyed a nationally representative sample of children aged 10 to 16. More than one in four (28.5%) of the children reported experiencing corporal punishment the year prior to the survey, 2.1% reported an attempted assault, and about 1 in 100 (0.9%) reported a completed assault by a parent in the previous year.

Sex and Age and Violence Toward Adolescents

Research findings depicting the relationship between sex and age of adolescents and the likelihood of violence and abuse are not always consistent. David Gil (1970), in his nationwide survey of child abuse, gathered information on abuse victims from cases reported through the central abuse registries in each state. Gil found only small differences between boys and girls at the younger ages, with boys being slightly more likely to be abused than girls. However, as children grow older, girls are more likely to be abused than boys. He attributed this finding to cultural attitudes regarding child-rearing practices in the United States. When children are younger, girls are more conforming than boys and require less discipline in the form of physical punishment. However, as children mature sexually, parents become more anxious over their daughters' heterosexual relationships. This anxiety leads to greater restrictions, increased conflict, and more frequent use of punishment to ensure parental control. With respect to boys, as they grow older, their physical strength increases and parents are less likely to use physical force for fear of retaliation. Also, the same anxieties that exist concerning the sexual activities of daughters do not exist for sons. Similarly, the national survey of reported and recognized maltreatment found that girls are much more likely to be abused and neglected than are boys (Burgdorf, 1980).

Other researchers have found the relationship between sex and age of adolescents and likelihood of abuse to be the exact opposite as that found by Gil. Straus and his colleagues (1980) found that young boys and girls were pushed, grabbed, shoved, slapped, and spanked at pretty much the same rate. But as they grew older, boys over the age of 10 were more likely to experience these forms of behavior than girls. Boys ages 15 to 17 were twice as likely as girls to be pushed, grabbed, or shoved. The higher rates of violence toward boys can be partially explained in terms of "linkage theory" (Straus, 1971), which states that parents socialize their children in accordance with the type of personality skills they feel their children will need later in life. If parents anticipate that their sons will be faced with aggressive situations more often than their daughters, parents will be more likely to use physical force toward their sons.

More recently, an analysis of data from the Second National Family Violence Survey (Wauchope & Straus, 1990) found no significant differences between adolescent boys and girls in terms of experiencing all forms of physical punishment. Finkelhor and Dziuba-Leatherman (1994a) also found no difference in experiencing assaults for boys and girls aged 10 to 16. Boys, however, were more likely to report experiencing corporal punishment at some time in their lives.

How can we explain the differences in the research findings concerning the age and sex of adolescents and their likelihood of abuse? Perhaps the answer lies in the techniques used by the researchers in collecting their information on abuse. Gil relied on child abuse cases reported to public officials in the 50 states. Similarly, the national survey of reported and recognized maltreatment is based on public perceptions and recognition of maltreatment. Straus, Gelles, Steinmetz, Finkelhor, and Dziuba-Leatherman all relied on self-reports of abuse. As has already been discussed in this book, the use of publicly identified cases of abuse has inherent problems. Perhaps girls were overrepresented in Gil's study because cases of abuse involving females were more likely to be reported to public officials than cases involving boys. Boys are taught to "be tough" and "don't cry" and thus may be more likely to conceal their inflicted injuries than girls.

The difference in findings may also be due to differences in the definition of abuse. Straus, Gelles, Steinmetz, Finkelhor, and Dziuba-Leatherman focused on violence without concern for whether an injury took place. Gil's definition of abuse was restricted to cases that produced an injury. Gil also studied many more forms of abusive violence (e.g., burning) than Straus and his colleagues. Perhaps females were more likely to be victims of the types of abuse not included in Straus and his colleagues' definition of victimization (such as strangling, drowning, burning, poisoning, or tying up or locking in).

Explaining Violence Toward Adolescents

Why are parents violent toward their adolescent children? One explanation is that they are violent and abusive toward their older children for the same reasons they are violent and abusive toward their younger children. In some instances, abuse of adolescents is an extension of violence that began when the teenager was a younger child. A second explanation is provided by Ira Lourie (1977), who points out that as children grow physically stronger and seek independence, parents may resort to more violent means of control. Another possible factor might be the struggle for independence between adolescents and their parents. Adolescence is a stressful period for children and parents. Last, parents see in their adolescent offspring the consequences of their parenting and may feel upset or guilty about their parent roles. Obviously, we need much more research on this issue to draw any kind of informed conclusion.

Parent Abuse

The idea of children attacking their parents is so foreign to our conceptions of parent-child relations that it is difficult for most of us to believe that such behavior occurs. Parents are granted the position of authority and power in the family's status hierarchy. Parents command control of the family's resources, such as money, power, status, and violence. According to the sociologist William Goode, violence is a legitimate resource at the disposal of family members, and it will be used whenever other attempts at alleviating a conflict fail. It is logically assumed, however, that the use of violence to resolve conflicts is brought into play by the typically dominant members of the family to ensure submission of those in their care. Goode argues that wives and children could, and sometimes do, use force but it does not occur frequently due to greater normative disapproval of children and wives using force against the father or husband.

> The rebellious child or wife knows the father or husband is stronger, and can call on outsiders who will support that force with more force. . . . The force or threat they command is not only their own strength but that of the community, which will back up the traditional family patterns. (Goode, 1971, pp. 625-626)

The societal attitudes concerning who uses violence within the family partially explains why this form of violence has been one of the least researched and consequently why, until recently, not very much was known about its extent, patterns, and causes.

Goode's (1971) quote alludes to other social attitudes that hinder recognition of parent abuse as a hidden form of family violence. Not only do children lack control of the family's resources, but they are also thought of as smaller and having less physical strength. This observation alone is enough to make us think that children are not physically capable of injuring their parents. However, what research is available graphically demonstrates that children can and do inflict injury on their parents. For example, one clinical study reports on the case of an 11-year-old boy who became aggressive toward his mother after she spanked him for dis-obeying orders. He reportedly pushed her down, broke her coccyx, and then proceeded to kick her in the face while she was on the floor (Harbin & Madden, 1979). Carol Warren (1978), in her investigation of 15 battering adolescents between the ages of 12 and 17 who were admitted to a psychiatric hospital, found that what these children lacked in physical strength, they more than made up for with speed and weapons. One 12-year-old "poured gasoline in the bathroom while his mother was in there, threw in a match, and shut the door" (p. 6). These examples demonstrate that physical size and strength are not always the best indicator as to who will be violent in a family.

Goode (1971) also quite accurately states that there is greater norma-tive disapproval of children using violence against a parent than of a parent using violence against their children. The community supports parental rights and obligations while imposing strong sanctions against children who violate traditional family patterns concerning the legitimate use of force. Children abusing their parents is so counter-normative that it is extremely difficult for parents to admit that they are being victimized by one of their children. Unless the children commit lethal acts or acts of extreme violence, it is rare that the behavior of violent children and adolescents comes to the public's attention. Discussion and reporting of such acts is almost a taboo subject because many parents are ashamed of their own victimization. Parents are afraid that others will blame them for their children's violent behavior. Parents of abusive children are believed to suffer from tremendous anxiety, depression, and guilt. Henry Harbin and Dennis Madden (1979) examined 15 families identified as having an adolescent between the ages of 14 and 20 who was assaulting a parent. All these families were trying desperately to maintain an illusion of family harmony. Parents would occasionally admit to being abused by their children immediately following a particularly aggressive episode, but the "veil of denial" would rapidly reappear. Parents would try endlessly to protect their abusive offspring. Harbin and Madden identified four ways in which the veil of denial and protection manifested itself: (a) the families would try to avoid all discussion of the violent episodes, (b) all the family members would attempt to minimize the seriousness of the aggressive behavior, (c) the parents would avoid punishment for the abusive behavior, and (d) the families refused to ask for outside help for either themselves or for their child. The role of denial and the creation of an image of a peaceful and loving family plays an important part in abusive families. This role allows the family to continue functioning even though the family must continually deny the reality of violence (Ferreira, 1963). Admission of violent behavior on the part of the offspring or the parent may introduce the threat of family separation. The denial of reality serves as a defense mechanism to protect the family from outside observers and influence.

Extent of Violence Toward Parents

The investigations of violence toward parents that have been conducted all report the same result: The rate of child-to-parent violence, although less than parent-to-child abuse, is large enough to warrant attention. The U.S. Department of Justice (1980) estimated that of the 1.2 million incidents of violence between relatives, 47,000 involved children's violence against parents. An examination of restraining order defendants in Massachusetts found that almost one third of all the restraining orders issued between September 1992 and June 1993 were requested by parents against their children (Cochran, Brown, Adams, & Doherty, 1994).

Surveys of adolescents and parents find rates of violence and abuse against parents ranging from 5% to 12%. Mulligan (1977) reports that 12% of the college students she questioned used at least one form of violence against a parent while they lived at home during their senior year of high school. Charles Peek and his colleagues (Peek, Fisher, & Kidwell, 1985) analyzed data collected from more than 1,500 parents of white male high school sophomores, juniors, and seniors as part of the Youth in Transition Survey. They found that between 7% and 11% of the parents reported being hit. Straus et al. (1980) found that 10% of the children 3 to 17 years of age in their sample performed at least one act of violence against a parent during a 1-year period (see Table 5.1). Our own statistics (Cornell & Gelles, 1982), generated from a nationally representative sample of families who had a teenager living at home between the ages of 10 and 17, agreed with the findings of the other studies—9% of parents reported at least one act of violence. This translates into approximately

TABLE 5.1   Incidence of Hidden Forms of Family Violence (in percentages)

Violent Acts	Sibling to Sibling	Parent to Adolescent	Adolescent to Parent
Any violence	82	46	9
Pushed or shoved	74	25	6
Slapped	48	28	3
Threw things	43	4	4
Kicked, bit, or punched	42	2	2
Hit or tried to hit with an object	40	7	2
Beat up	16	1.3	0.7
Threatened with a knife or gun	0.8	0.2	0.3
Used a knife or gun	0.3	0.2	0.2

SOURCE: Based on data from Straus et al. (1980).

2.5 million parents being struck at least once a year. A statistic was also calculated for the more severe forms of violence. Approximately 3% of the adolescents were reported to have kicked, punched, bit, beat up, or used a knife or gun against a parent. Although this percentage appears quite small, when it is projected to the total number of adolescents between ages 10 and 17 living in two-parent households, it means that 900,000 parents are being abused each year. Robert Agnew and Sandra Huguley (1989) analyzed data from the 1972 National Survey of Youth and reported that roughly 5% of the adolescents in the survey hit one of their parents in the previous year.

Children not only hit and assault their parents, they kill them as well. A National Institute of Justice analysis of murder victims and defendants in the 75 largest urban counties in the United States found that 2% of all family murder victims were parents killed by their children (Dawson & Langan, 1994). For the period 1977 to 1986, approximately 1 of 11 family homicides nationwide were parents killed by their children (Heide, 1989).

Some of the cases of children killing their parents have generated enormous publicity. The most recent case is that of the Menendez brothers in Los Angeles, who were convicted of the shotgun killings of their parents. In this case, as in others, such as Richard and Deborah Jahnke in Wyoming or Cheryl Pierson on Long Island, New York, the children claimed that the killings were the result of years of physical, emotional, or sexual abuse at the hands of their parents.

Factors Related to Violence Toward Parents

Who is violent? Harbin and Madden (1979) found that the majority of children who attack a parent are between the ages of 13 and 24, although they also report on children as young as 10 years old inflicting injury on their parents. Researchers agree that sons are slightly more likely to be violent and abusive than daughters. In Massachusetts, nearly two thirds (64%) of the restraining orders in parent abuse cases were issued for mothers against their sons (Cochran et al., 1994).

Sons' rates of severe violence against a parent appears to increase with age, whereas for daughters the rates of severe violence decline with age. Agnew and Huguley (1989) found that as boys grew older, they were somewhat less likely to hit their mothers and more likely to hit their fathers. This suggests, perhaps, that boys do take advantage of increased size and strength that comes with adolescent growth. A social explanation could be that the boys and girls are adhering to the cultural norms that reward aggressiveness in teenage boys but negatively sanction the use of violence among teenage girls.

Irrespective of who is the victim of a parricide—mother, father, stepfather, or stepmother—sons are overwhelmingly the killers. More than 85% of the offenders in parricide are sons (Heide, 1989, 1995).

Researchers generally found that mothers are more likely to be hit and assaulted than fathers (Cornell & Gelles, 1982; U.S. Department of Justice, 1994a). An examination of police reports of formal complaints about adolescent aggression toward parents found that the modal pattern was male adolescent violence toward mothers (Evans & Warren-Sohlberg, 1988). Finally, a survey of adolescents concludes that mothers are more likely to be victims of their children's violence but that fathers are the more likely victims of older male children (Agnew & Huguley, 1989).

Whereas mothers are more likely to be hit by their children than are fathers, fathers, whether biological or stepfathers, are more likely to be killed by their children who are under the age of 30 than are mothers or stepmothers. If the offender is over 30 years old, the victim is more likely to be the mother or stepmother as opposed to the father or stepfather (Heide, 1989, 1995).

Clinical observations of adolescents who had abused a parent found that most families had some disturbance in the authority structure within the family. Adolescents had been granted too much control. Abused parents seemed to be turning to young or immature children for decision making. This tremendous responsibility on the shoulders of young people seemed to generate extreme frustration. Harbin and Madden (1979) claim that the physical attacks on the parent were often an attempt by the adolescents to either control the family or to punish the parents for placing them in the decision-making role in the first place. Many of the abusive children had very poor self-concepts; whenever they were challenged or made to feel insecure, anxiety was created, often resulting in violent episodes.

In those instances when children, especially adolescent children, kill their parents, the key underlying factor is that the child has been severely abused (Heide, 1995; Mones, 1991). In a smaller number of cases of parricide, the child is severely mentally ill or has an antisocial personality disorder (Heide, 1995).

Although child abuse and spouse abuse have been found to be related to many social, family structural, and situational factors, adolescent violence does not seem to vary in any meaningful way with these same factors. Adolescent violence cannot be explained using the same social factors that explain adult violence. The data do appear to indicate, as noted in the previous paragraph, that the rates of parent abuse are related to the frequency of other forms of family violence in the home. The more violence children experience or witness, the more likely they are to strike out at a parent. These findings are consistent with the theory that families who view violence as a legitimate way to resolve conflict run a greater risk of experiencing all forms of family violence, including parent abuse. Adolescents who have friends who assault parents, who approve of delinquency under certain conditions, who perceive the possibility of being arrested as low, and who are weakly attached to their parents have been found to be the most likely to use violence toward their parents (Agnew & Huguley, 1989).

Elder Abuse

Abuse of elders is the only form of hidden family violence that has generated a significant amount of professional and public concern; yet abuse of elders still remains a poorly understood facet of intimate violence. In part, this is because the study of elder abuse is a recent development. Prior to the 1980s, elder abuse received about as much social recognition as parent abuse, adolescent abuse, and sibling violence. There are several easily identifiable factors that can help explain society's recent interest in this topic. Major demographic changes, which have occurred over the past half century, have increased the number of older Americans in our population. This is a direct result of the life expectancy of the average person increasing by nearly 50% in approximately 50 years (U.S. Bureau of the Census, 1995). As people lived longer and the fertility rate declined in the 1970s and 1980s, the proportion of older people in the population also increased. This growing number of older Americans has heightened our awareness of the many problems being experienced by elders. These changes have, in turn, had an effect on family responsibilities. As people live longer, there is a growing need for middle-aged children to share the responsibility of caring for an aged parent. Of those between 65 and 72 years of age, only 1 elderly person in 50 needs long-term care. But among those 73 years of age and over, the numbers increase to 1 in 15 (Koch & Koch, 1980). Children having the responsibility of caring for their aging parents is also a relatively new and growing aspect of family life. For these reasons, researchers have become interested in studying the consequences of caring for aging parents in the home. They realize that it is impractical to expect all families to have the appropriate financial, emotional, and social resources to handle this additional burden.

The recognition of elder abuse as a social problem and the subsequent identification of abuse victims have not been easy tasks. Many obstacles have stood in the way. To begin with, elders are not tied in to many social networks, such as mandatory schooling or employment, that facilitate easier identification of victims. Elders are, on average, even more isolated from the mainstream of society than are younger adults. This isolation allows violent behavior to continue unimpeded, with elderly victims sometimes confined to their homes, sometimes dependent on those who are abusing them. Identification of abuse victims is also hindered by elderly victims' unwillingness to report incidents of maltreatment to the authorities. Karl Pillemer and David Finkelhor (1988) estimate that only 1 in 14 cases of abuse come to the attention of authorities. Sometimes friends, relatives, or neighbors are aware of what is happening but they are frightened and unsure of what to do. In the majority of cases, however, elder abuse becomes known to the authorities through a third party, typically someone who provides social or health care services to elders

(Tatara, 1993b). Even after the occurrence of abuse has been reported and substantiated, many abuse victims are unwilling to admit to it.

According to Toshio Tatara's (1993b) examination of reports of elder abuse to state adult protective services agencies, only about 5% of elder abuse reports are made by the elders themselves. There are a number of reasons to explain the victims' hesitancy to report their own abuse and neglect. Due to societal attitudes, many elderly family members are too embarrassed to admit that they have raised a child capable of such behavior. Again, as with other forms of family violence, they assume the blame for their abuser's behavior. Frequently, their love for their abuser is stronger than the desire to leave the abusive situation. They are more concerned for the welfare of their abuser than for their own safety and well-being. They are unwilling to begin any legal action that might result in some sort of punishment for their abuser, and consequently, they further their own isolation. This fear of isolation is a result of the majority of victims living in the same house as their abuser (Legal Research and Services for the Elderly, 1979). Those elderly people who are physically, emotionally, or economically dependent on their abusers may be unsure of what alternatives are available to them if they do report the abuse. An important problem is that the alternatives available to aged family members who may wish to leave an abusive environment are often considered worse than the abusive situation. In particular, the elderly victim often considers institutionalized care as the worst possible alternative. This fear of institutionalization is apparently a valid one. A study of abuse victims reported to the Cleveland Chronic Illness Center found that 46% of the cases of elder abuse eventually resulted in institutionalization of the victim (Lau & Kosberg, 1979). In 26% of the cases, assistance was refused by the victim and in 28% of the cases assistance other than institutionalization was offered and accepted.

Another factor that hinders identification of abuse victims is the low level of awareness among public service agencies regarding the issue of elder abuse. Agencies dealing with elders were initially very reluctant to become involved in abuse cases. They were concerned about violations of confidentiality. When the issue of confidentiality had been resolved, the agencies often did not have the personnel and resources available to effectively handle reported cases. It has been noted that these were precisely the same issues that hindered action in the identification, awareness, and treatment of child abuse 20 years earlier (Rathbone-McCuan, 1980).

Nature and Extent of Elder Abuse

Abusive treatment toward elders can take many forms. Caretakers may tie an aged relative to a bed or chair while they go out shopping or finish their housework. They may overmedicate their parents to "ease" the older person's discomfort and to make them more manageable. Other caretakers resort to physical attacks to "make them mind" or to coerce their elderly relatives into changing a will or signing the house deed or social security checks over to them. Some caretakers have used such excessive physical violence or have neglected the needs of the older person to such an extent that death has resulted.

The varied forms of the mistreatment of elders are typically grouped into four categories: (a) *physical abuse*, the infliction of physical pain or injury, including punching, bruising, restraining, or sexually molesting; (b) *psychological abuse*, the infliction of mental anguish, such as humiliating, intimidating, and threatening harm; (c) *financial abuse*, the illegal or improper exploitation of the elder's property or assets; and (d) *neglect*, including refusal or deliberate failure to fulfill a caretaking obligation, such as abandoning the elder or denial of food or health care. Some definitions of elder abuse include a fifth category of *self-abuse*, where the harm is inflicted by the elder him- or herself.

As with child maltreatment, the forms of elder abuse include acts of commission (physical abuse) and omission (neglect). And as with child maltreatment, there is no consensus among researchers, service providers, governmental agencies, or legal experts as to what the appropriate definition of elder abuse should be. And as with child maltreatment, the variation of definitions has produced varying estimates of the extent of elder abuse.

Estimates of the proportion of those 65 years of age or older who are abused or neglected range from 4% to 10% (Pagelow, 1989). Rosalie Wolf (1995) estimates that 5% of those 65 years of age or older are victims of physical abuse, psychological abuse, financial exploitation, and/or neglect in the previous year. A rate of 5% would mean that 2 million elders 65 years of age or older are abused each year.

One of the responses to the increasing recognition of elder abuse is that states enacted reporting laws for elder abuse, along the lines of mandatory reporting laws for child maltreatment. Forty-two states and the District of Columbia have enacted mandatory reporting laws (Wolf, 1995). Tatara (1993b) has surveyed state departments of adult protective services in an attempt to measure the number of cases of elder abuse and neglect that are reported each year. A 1992 survey received responses from 74 different agencies from 52 jurisdictions, representing 49 states and the District of Columbia (Tatara, 1993b). During 1991, these agencies received 227,000 reports representing 206,000 individual alleged victims of mistreatment. As with child maltreatment, not all reports are deemed valid after investigation. In 1991, 54.6% of the reports were substantiated by the investigating agency. Reports increased to 241,000 in 1994 and 59.9% were substantiated (National Center on Elder Abuse, 1995).

More than half of the substantiated cases of elder abuse were self-neglect; thus, the total number of substantiated cases of elder abuse that involved acts of those other than the victim was 65,106 (National Center on Elder Abuse, 1995). Of those cases where a perpetrator could be identified, 58.4% involved neglect; 15.4%, physical abuse; and 12.3%, financial exploitation.

As with other forms of intimate violence, only a portion of instances of physical abuse or sexual abuse comes to the attention of official agencies. Thus, estimates of the extent of elder abuse based on officially reported cases are underestimates of the actual extent of the abuse of elders. Pillemer and Finkelhor (1988) conducted the first large-scale random sample survey of elder abuse and neglect. Interviews were conducted with 2,020 community-dwelling (noninstitutionalized) elderly persons in the Boston metropolitan area. Overall, 32 elderly persons per 1,000 reported experiencing some form of maltreatment, including physical violence, verbal aggression, and/or neglect in the past year. The rate of physical violence was 20 per 1,000. Although the conventional view of elder abuse is that of middle-aged children abusing and neglecting their elderly parents, Pillemer and Finkelhor found that spouses were the most frequent abusers of elders and that roughly equal numbers of men and women were victims. Women, however, suffered from the most serious forms of abuse. Daughter-to-father violence is the rarest form of abuse, and son-to-mother or son-to-father is the most common form.

Similar results to the Pillemer and Finkelhor survey were found in a self-report survey conducted in Canada, although the rate of each specific form of abuse is lower in Canada than in the Boston study (Podnieks, 1992). Surveys in Great Britain and Finland also find rates of maltreatment of about 5% (Kivela, Kongas-Saviaro, Kesti, Pahkala, & Ijas, 1992; Ogg & Bennett, 1992).

Factors Related to Elder Abuse

Based on the existing data, the most likely victim of elder abuse is a female of very advanced age (Pillemer & Frankel, 1991). One of the most commonly cited causal factors in the elder abuse literature is the resentment generated by the dependency of an older person on a caretaker. Research reports that victims of elder abuse often suffer from physical and/or mental impairments and are dependent on their caretakers for many, if not most, of their daily needs (Block & Sinnott, 1979; Legal Research and Services for the Elderly, 1979; Rathbone-McCuan, 1980; Steinmetz, 1978c, 1993). It is this dependent situation of elders that is believed to increase their likelihood of being abused. Suzanne Steinmetz (1978c) notes that several parallels exist between child abuse and elder abuse. Both children and elders are in dependent positions in the family and rely on their caregivers for the provision of basic needs. Both are presumed to be protected and adequately cared for within the family setting, and both can become a source of economic, physical, or emotional strain. Steinmetz believes that although most couples expect to care for children, they do not always anticipate the possibility of caring for their aged parents. The process of caring for elderly parents presents unique problems for any family. Whereas children become less and less dependent with age, the health of aging relatives renders them more and more dependent.

Other researchers have found that it is the dependency of the abusers and not the elders that is a risk factor for elder abuse (Hwalek, Senstock, & Lawrence, 1984; Pillemer, 1985, 1993; Wolf, Strugnell, & Godkin, 1982). Especially in cases of physical abuse, the perpetrators tend to be financially and emotionally dependent on those they abuse. The explanation for this contradiction to the commonsense explanation for the occurrence of elder abuse is that abuse is an act carried out as a response to perceived powerlessness (Finkelhor, 1983). The adult child who is still dependent on an elderly parent may strike out or maltreat as a compensation for the lack, or loss, of power.

There are other risk factors related to abuse of elders in addition to dependence of the abuser or abused. There is some suggestion that stressful events increase the risk of abuse, but there are only a handful of studies that actually rigorously assess the effect of external stress on the likelihood of abuse (Pillemer & Frankel, 1991). As with other forms of violence and abuse, abused elders tend to be more socially isolated than are nonabused elders (Phillips, 1983; Pillemer, 1986). Although the intergenerational cycle of violence is thought to be part of the risk profile of other forms of intimate violence, there is as yet no research that documents that parents who abused their children are likely to be abused by those same children in later life compared to parents who have not abused their children (Pillemer & Frankel, 1991).

Violence in Gay and Lesbian Relationships

The most overlooked form of intimate violence is violence in gay and lesbian relationships. In the 1970s and 1980s, the use of the term *family violence* resulted in a focus on violence that occurred within traditional, heterosexual marriages. The term *intimate violence* allowed for the expanding the focus on violence to nonmarital relationships. The feminist theoretical perspective (see Chapter 6) conceptualized intimate violence as something men do mostly to women. Traditional services for treating intimate violence were shelters for women who were victimized by men, arrest for male batterers, and treatment groups for violent men. Primary prevention efforts aimed at confronting and changing cultural values that supported male domination of women. Cultural attitudes about gays and lesbians, including homophobic attitudes and behavior, constrained victims of gay and lesbian violence from speaking out about their victimization. Thus, until quite recently, victims of gay and lesbian violence were nearly invisible, except to the clinicians in whom the victims confided about both their homosexuality and their abusive treatment at the hands of their partners.

Extent of Gay and Lesbian Violence

There have been a few recent examinations of the extent of gay and lesbian violence. These are typically studies of small, nonprobability samples (Brand & Kidd, 1986; Renzetti, 1992). These and other studies indicate that the incidence of violence in same-sex couples ranges from 11% to more than 45%. Although it is impossible to compare these data to studies of heterosexual intimate violence based on nationally representative samples, it appears that the extent of violence in gay and lesbian relationships is at least as high as violence in heterosexual couples, if not higher.

As with violence in heterosexual couples, violence among gays and lesbians is not a rare, one-time event. Claire Renzetti (1992) found that 8% of the 100 lesbians she interviewed had experienced one or two abusive incidents, while 54% had experienced 10 or more incidents in the course of the relationship. The violence in gay and lesbian couples includes physical violence, injury-producing violence, and emotional and sexual abuse. One distinct aspect of emotional abuse may include "outing" the partner (Renzetti, 1995).

Patterns of Gay and Lesbian Violence

If violence in gay and lesbian relationships is recognized at all, there is the assumption that the nature of the violence conforms to stereotypical roles that gays and lesbians are believed to play in relationships. Thus, the offender in the lesbian couple is believed to be the masculine or "butch" partner, and the victim is the "fem" or feminine partner. Renzetti (1995) reports that the available data on gay and lesbian violence demonstrates that stereotypical sex roles or physical size are not related to offender and victim roles. Researchers also believe that although the partners are same sex, there is no pattern of prevalent mutual violence in gay and lesbian relations (Letellier, 1994; Renzetti, 1992).

Although the available research on gay and lesbian violence is limited, those who have examined psychological and physical abuse explain that as with violence in heterosexual couples, power and power imbalances are key triggers to the occurrence of gay and lesbian violence (Lockhart, White, Causby, & Isaac, 1994). It is presumed that egalitarian lesbian and gay relationships have lower levels of violence compared with couples with greater resource and power imbalances.

Program and Policy Challenges

Clearly, the major policy and program challenge of gay and lesbian couple violence is the virtual invisibility of the offenders and victims.

Service providers need to overcome homophobic beliefs and attitudes. They also need to overcome assumptions that include assuming that gay and lesbians have nonviolent relationships and that when violence does occur it conforms to stereotypical sex roles. Finally, there are unique dilemmas that occur, such as when both the offender and victim of lesbian violence simultaneously seek services from the same shelter or agency.

We need much more research on violence in gay and lesbian relationships if we are to understand this facet of intimate violence, provide appropriate services, and develop effective social policies.

Summary

It is quite clear that the rates of hidden forms of intimate violence are as high or higher than the better-known types of violence. Our understanding of the hidden victims of violence is limited because there has been very little research on these forms of violence. The data on sibling violence and violence toward parents are either anecdotal or come from small, local studies (with the exception of Straus and his colleagues' National Family Violence Survey). Data on elder abuse are also limited, although we now have an improved national tally of reported cases of elder abuse. And in the near future, there will be a national incidence study of elder abuse designed along the lines of the National Center on Child Abuse and Neglect survey of recognized and reported cases of child maltreatment.

It is hoped that conceptualizing the problem as one of *intimate* violence will lead to more recognition and research on the hidden forms of intimate violence and a better understanding of all forms of intimate violence. A perspective that recognizes that all intimate relationships can be and sometimes are violent might help us broaden our examination into the generative sources of intimate violence. The next chapter attempts to apply that broader perspective and poses a general theory of intimate violence.

DISCUSSION QUESTIONS

1. Why have the hidden forms of intimate violence been overlooked? How does blaming the victim contribute to keeping certain forms of intimate violence hidden? How do cultural norms and values concerning children, parents, elders, gay men, and lesbians contribute to keeping certain forms of intimate violence hidden?

2. Why has elder abuse received more attention than the other forms of hidden violence?

3. What are some of the factors related to hidden forms of violence? How do the factors related to hidden violence compare to factors related to the abuse of young children or violence between spouses?

SUGGESTED ASSIGNMENTS

1. Find out if your state has mandatory reporting laws for cases of elder abuse. Who is required to report? How many cases are reported each year? Has there been an increase in reporting in the past few years? What services are available in your community, city, or state for victims of elder abuse?

2. Conduct a survey and measure people's awareness of and attitudes toward the known forms of family violence (child abuse or wife abuse) and the hidden forms. Be sure to ask parallel questions so that you can compare the results.

3. Interview staff at a shelter for battered women and ask them about whether they encounter instances of lesbian violence and what services they provide for victims of violence in lesbian relationships. Ask if they have policies for dealing with the situation when both victim and offender seek services from the shelter.

6

EXPLAINING INTIMATE AND FAMILY VIOLENCE

The discussions in previous chapters about the factors that are related to various types of intimate violence shed some light on our understanding of why parents batter children, husbands abuse wives, and other family members assault their siblings and parents. Nevertheless, a list of factors associated with family violence still does not complete our understanding. People with low incomes may be more likely to abuse a family member, but income is not a complete explanation of family violence.

This chapter expands our analysis of intimate and family violence by asking the question, Why is the family such a violent institution? The answer can be found by looking at some of the unique characteristics of the family as a social group. Next, I review the major theories that have been used to explain family and intimate violence, and I conclude with an integrated exchange/social control explanation.

Violence and the Organization of Family Life

For much of this book, I have concentrated on examining the characteristics of individuals and families and intimate relations and how these characteristics are related to various types of family and intimate violence. To concentrate only on individuals and family relations would, to a certain extent, miss the forest for the trees. Although many people consider the most important questions in the study of family violence to be, Who are the abusive family members and why are they abusive? another equally important question is, Why are families and intimate relationships so violent? Once we have completed our examination of the incidence and extent of the various types of family violence, we are left with the quite inescapable conclusion that the family is society's most violent institution, excepting only the military in times of war. Why is the family the place where you are the most likely to be killed, physically assaulted, hit, beat up, slapped, or spanked? Until we consider the social organization of the family that makes it violence prone, we have not adequately addressed the questions with which we opened this book.

Richard Gelles and Murray Straus (1979) identified the unique characteristics of the family as a social group that contribute to making the family a violence-prone institution. Later, Straus, with his colleague Gerald Hotaling (1979), noted the irony that these same characteristics we saw as making the family violence prone also serve to make the family a warm, supportive, and intimate environment. Briefly, these factors are the following:

1. *Time at risk.* The ratio of time spent interacting with family members and intimates far exceeds the ratio of time spent interacting with others, although the ratio will vary depending on stages in the family life cycle.

2. *Range of activities and interests.* Not only do family members and intimates spend a great deal of time with one another, the interaction ranges over a much wider spectrum of activities than nonfamilial interaction.

3. *Intensity of involvement.* The quality of family and intimate interaction is also unique. The degree of commitment to family interaction is greater. A cutting remark made by a family member or an intimate partner is likely to have a much greater effect than the same remark in another setting or by someone else.

4. *Impinging activities.* Many interactions in the family and in intimate relationships are inherently conflict structured and have a "zero-sum" aspect. Whether it involves deciding what television show to watch or what car to buy, there will be both winners and losers in intimate relations.

5. *Right to influence.* Belonging to a family carries with it the implicit right to influence the values, attitudes, and behaviors of other family members.

6. *Age and sex differences.* The family is unique in that it is made up of different ages and sexes. Thus, there is the potential for battles between generations and sexes.

7. *Ascribed roles.* In addition to the problem of age and sex differences is the fact that the family is perhaps the only social institution that assigns roles and responsibilities based on age and sex rather than interest or competence.

8. *Privacy.* The modern family is a private institution, insulated from the eyes, ears, and often rules of the wider society. Where privacy is high, the degree of social control will be low.

9. *Involuntary membership.* Families are exclusive organizations. Birth relationships are involuntary and cannot be terminated. Whereas there can be ex-wives and ex-husbands, there are no ex-children or ex-parents. Being in a family involves personal, social, material, and legal commitment and entrapment. When conflict arises, it is not easy to break off the conflict by fleeing the scene or resigning from the group.

10. *Stress.* Families are prone to stress. This is due in part to the theoretical notion that dyadic relationships are unstable (Simmel, 1950). Moreover, families are constantly undergoing changes and transitions. The birth of children, maturation of children, aging, retirement, and death are all changes recognized by family scholars. Moreover, stress felt by one family member (such as unemployment, illness, bad grades at school) is transmitted to other family members.

11. *Extensive knowledge of social biographies.* The intimacy and emotional involvement of family and intimate relations reveal a full range of identities to members of a family. Strengths and vulnerabilities, likes and dislikes, loves and fears are all known to family members. Although this knowledge can help support a relationship, the information can also be used to attack intimates and lead to conflict.

It is one thing to say that the social organization of the family makes it a conflict-prone institution and social group. However, the 11 characteristics I listed do not supply the total answer. The key additional consideration is one I discussed in Chapter 2. The fact that the social organization of the family I have just described exists within a cultural context where violence is tolerated, accepted, and even mandated is a critical factor that helps us understand why the family, as currently structured, can be loving, supportive, and violent. The widespread acceptability of physical punishment to raise children creates a situation where a conflict-prone institution serves as a training ground to teach children that it is acceptable (a) to hit people you love, (b) for powerful people to hit less powerful people, (c) to use hitting to achieve some end or goal, and (d) to hit as an end in itself (Straus, 1994).

Theories That Explain Intimate Violence

Psychiatric/Personality Theory

Although I discussed the psychiatric model previously and have found that this explanation for family violence is limited, its popularity in the professional literature as well as among the general public causes me to repeat the model and its problems one more time.

The tragic picture of a defenseless child, woman, or grandparent subjected to abuse and neglect arouses the strongest emotions in clinicians and others who see and treat the problem of intimate violence. There frequently seems to be no rational explanation for harming a loved one. It is not surprising, therefore, that a psychiatric model of family violence was the first applied to the problem and has endured for years. Even sociologists can find themselves using such a model. Once I was working in a clinic at Children's Hospital of Boston. We were examining and doing a psycho-social-medical evaluation of a young child who had suffered a severe immersion burn (she had been forced into a bathtub filled with scalding hot water). It was obvious that she had been purposely burned, because she had been pressed against the tub with such force that neither the soles of her feet nor her bottom had been burned. After the scalding, she had apparently been tied to the bed and this had resulted in lacerations of her wrists and ankles. After our examination, we returned to our offices and wrote up our clinic notes. My colleague, Eli Newberger, came by and asked me what I thought about the case. I responded, "Anyone who would do that is crazy!" Eli looked puzzled. "Aren't you the person who wrote in 1973 that the psychopathological model of abuse was a myth?" he asked me. (I did, and my model is presented in Chapter 3.) "I don't care what I wrote," I responded, "I know what I saw!"

The psychiatric model focuses on the abuser's personality characteristics as the chief determinants of violence and abuse. A psychiatric model links factors such as mental illness, personality defects, psycho-pathology, sociopathology, alcohol and drug misuse, or other intra-individual abnormalities to family violence. A number of studies have found a high incidence of psychopathology among abusive individuals (Hamberger & Hastings, 1986, 1991; Hart, Dutton, & Newlove, 1993; Hastings & Hamberger, 1988).

The psychologist Donald Dutton (Dutton & Golant, 1995; Dutton & Starzomski, 1993) has developed a psychological profile and explanation of men who batter their wives (1995). Dutton's psychological profile applies to what he calls cyclical batterers (see Chapter 4 of this book), whose cyclical moods ebb and flow as does their violent behavior. Dutton argues that cyclical abusers are characterized by having borderline personalities—that is, their personality type is on the border between psychotics and neurotics. Dutton explains that this personality is devel-oped early in life. Abusive men have deep-seated feelings of power-lessness that have their origins in the man's early development. Abusive men tend to have shaming, emotionally rejecting, or absent fathers and are left in the arms of a mother who is only intermittently available but who the boy perceives as all powerful. According to Dutton, these boys never recover from these early traumas (Dutton & Golant, 1995, p. 121).

Although Dutton believes that there is a common psychological profile of batterers, other researchers argue that less than 10% of instances of family violence is attributable solely to personality traits, mental illness, or psychopathology (Steele, 1978; Straus, 1980).

In closing this discussion, it is important to speculate why people persist in applying the psychiatric model to more cases of family violence than is warranted. The answer may lie, paradoxically, in the fact that intimate violence is so extensive in our society that we do not want to recognize it as a pattern of family relations. Somehow, we do not want to consider our own potential to abuse or even to consider that some of the acts we engage in (pushing a wife, slapping a child) are violent or abusive. If we can persist in believing that violence and abuse are the products of aberrations or sickness, and if we believe ourselves to be well, then our acts cannot be hurtful or abusive. Furthermore, the psychiatric model serves as an ideal smokescreen to blind us from considering social orga-nizational factors that cause family violence.

Social-Situational/Stress and Coping Theory

That personality problems and psychopathology do not fully explain acts of family violence does not mean that personal problems are unrelated to intimate abuse. These personal problems, however, tend to arise from social antecedents. I have reviewed in previous chapters those social factors such as conflict, unemployment, isolation, unwanted pregnancy, and stress.

A social-situational/stress and coping theory of family violence proposes that abuse and violence arise out of two main factors. The first is structural stress. The association between low income and family violence, for instance, indicates that a central factor in violence and abuse is inadequate financial resources. The second main factor is the cultural norm concerning force and violence in the home (see Chapter 2). "Spare the rod and spoil the child." "The marriage license is a hitting license." These are phrases that underscore the widespread social approval for the use of force and violence at home.

The social-situational/stress and coping theory notes that such structural stresses as low income, unemployment, limited educational resources, illness, and the like are unevenly distributed in society. Although members in all families are told that they should be loving parents, adoring husbands, and caring wives, only some families get sufficient resources to meet these demands. Others fall considerably short of being able to have the psychological, social, and economic resources to meet the expectations of society, friends, neighbors, loved ones, and themselves. Combined with the cultural approval for violence, these shortfalls lead many family members and intimates to adopt violence and abuse as a means of coping with structural stress.

Social Learning Theory

A commonly stated explanation for family and intimate violence is that people learn to be violent when they grow up in violent homes. The family is the first place where people learn the roles of mother and father, husband and wife. The family is one key place where we learn how to cope with stress and frustration. The family is also the place where people are most likely to first experience violence. We have seen already in previous chapters that violence is frequently transmitted from generation to generation. Again, we must warn that not all violence victims grow up to be violent themselves. But a history of abuse and violence does increase the risk that an individual will be violent as an adult.

Individuals are not only exposed to techniques of being violent, but they also learn the social and moral justifications for the behavior. It is not uncommon to hear parents who have physically struck their own children explain that they were punishing the children for the children's own good. We have interviewed many parents who use exactly the same physical punishment on their children that they themselves experienced (some even use the exact same objects, passed down from generation to generation).

Resource Theory

Another explanation of family violence that is supported by the available scientific data is resource theory (Goode, 1971). This model assumes that all social systems (including the family) rest to some degree on force or the threat of force. The more resources—social, personal, and economic—a person can command, the more force he or she can muster. However, according to William Goode, the author of this theory, the more resources a person actually has, the less he or she will actually use force in an open manner. Thus, a husband who wants to be the dominant person in the family, but has little education, has a job low in prestige and income, and lacks interpersonal skills, may choose to use violence to maintain the dominant position. In addition, family members (including children) may use violence to redress a grievance when they have few alternative resources available.

An Ecological Perspective

The ecological perspective is an attempt to integrate three levels of theoretical analysis (individual, social-psychological, and sociocultural) into a single theoretical model. James Garbarino (1977) and Jay Belsky (1980, 1993) have proposed an ecological model to explain the complex nature of child maltreatment. The model rests on three levels of analysis: the relationship between the organism and environment, the interacting and overlapping systems in which human development occurs, and environmental quality. The ecological model proposes that violence and

abuse arise out of a mismatch of parent to child and family to neighborhood and community. The risk of abuse and violence is greatest when
the functioning of the children and parents is limited and constrained by
developmental problems. Children with learning disabilities and social or
emotional handicaps are at increased risk for abuse. Parents under considerable stress, or who have personality problems, are at increased risk
for abusing their children. These conditions are worsened when social
interaction between the spouses or the parents and children heighten the
stress or make the personal problems worse. Finally, if there are few
institutions and agencies in the community to support troubled families,
then the risk of abuse is further raised. Garbarino (1977) identifies two
necessary conditions for child maltreatment. First, there must be cultural
justification for the use of force against children. Second, the maltreating
family is isolated from potent family or community support systems. The
ecological model has served as a perspective to examine other forms of
family violence. However, the model has mostly served to organize thinking and research about family violence. There has not yet been an actual
test of the integrated model, other than the research conducted by
Garbarino in the 1970s.

Sociobiology Theory

A sociobiological, or evolutionary, perspective of family violence
suggests that violence toward human or nonhuman primate offspring is
the result of the reproductive success potential of children and parental
investment. The theory's central assumption is that natural selection is the
process of differential reproduction and reproductive success (Daly &
Wilson, 1980). Males can be expected to invest in offspring when there is
some degree of parental certainty (how confident the father is that the child
is his own genetic offspring), whereas females are also inclined to invest
under conditions of parental certainty. Parents recognize their offspring
and avoid squandering valuable reproductive effort on someone else's
offspring. Children not genetically related to the parent (e.g., stepchildren, adopted, or foster children) or children with low reproductive
potential (e.g., handicapped or retarded children) are at the highest risk
for infanticide and abuse (Burgess & Garbarino, 1983; Daly & Wilson,
1980; Hrdy, 1979). Large families can dilute parental energy and lower
attachment to children, thus increasing the risk of child abuse and neglect
(Burgess, 1979).

Barbara Smuts (1992) applied an evolutionary perspective to male aggression against females. Smuts explains that male aggression against females often reflects male reproductive striving. Both human and nonhuman male primates are believed to use aggression against females to intimidate females so that they will not resist future male efforts to mate with them and to reduce the likelihood that females will mate with other males. Thus, males use aggression to control female sexuality to males' reproductive advantage. The frequency of male aggression varies across societies and situations depending on the strength of female alliances, the support women can receive from their families, the strength and importance of male alliances, the degree of equality in male-female relationships, and the degree to which males control the economic resources within a society. Male aggression toward females, both physical violence and rape, is high when female alliances are weak, when females lack kin support, when male alliances are strong, when male-female relationships are unbalanced, and when males control societal resources.

A Model of Sexual Abuse

David Finkelhor (1984) has reviewed research on the factors that have been proposed as contributing to sexual abuse of children and has developed what he calls a four-precondition model of sexual abuse (see Figure 6.1). His review suggests that all the factors relating to sexual abuse can be grouped into one of four preconditions that need to be met before sexual abuse can occur:

1. A potential offender needs to have some motivation to abuse a child sexually.
2. The potential offender has to overcome internal inhibitions against acting on that motivation.
3. The potential offender has to overcome external impediments to committing sexual abuse.
4. The potential offender or some other factor has to undermine or overcome a child's possible resistance to sexual abuse.

Feminist Theory

Feminist theorists and researchers (e.g., Dobash & Dobash, 1979; Pagelow, 1984; Smith, 1991a, 1991b; Yllö, 1983, 1988, 1993) see wife abuse as a unique phenomenon more closely aligned with other forms of

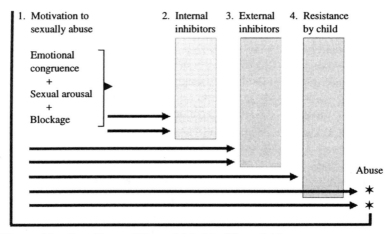

Figure 6.1. Four Preconditions: A Model of Sexual Abuse
SOURCE: Reprinted with the permission of The Free Press, a division of Simon & Schuster, from *Child Sexual Abuse: New Theory and Research*, by David Finkelhor. Copyright © 1984 by David Finkelhor.

violence against women (such as rape and sexual assault) than with child abuse and nonmarital forms of elder abuse. The central thesis of this theory is that economic, social, and historical processes operate directly and indirectly to support patriarchal (male dominated) social order and family structure. Patriarchy is seen as leading to the subordination of women, and wife beating is one of the mechanisms for maintaining this subordination. As with all forms of oppression, patriarchal means of control are often subtle and deeply entrenched, with the most violent forms not emerging until and unless patriarchal control is threatened—as when individual women leave or threaten to leave relationships or groups of women assert their rights (Campbell, 1992; Counts, Brown, & Campbell, 1992; Stark & Flitcraft, 1996).

An Exchange/Social Control
Theory of Intimate Violence

Some time ago, I was called by a newspaper reporter who was writing an editorial on family violence. He wanted me to give him a short one- or two-sentence statement on why family members used violence on one another. At first, the thought of boiling down many years of research into a sound bite seemed impossible. But I had been wrestling for some time with a project that was aimed at developing an integrated theory of family violence. I wanted a theory that was applicable to child abuse, wife abuse, and the hidden forms of intimate violence. One attempt to develop an integrated theory failed miserably when the resulting model was so complex that even I had a hard time following it when I had to proofread the figure for a book in which it was to be published. Although I wanted to integrate the best and most useful elements from the theories I reviewed, this seemed to be impossible.

As a consequence, I turned to trying to develop a more "middle-range" (Merton, 1945) theory. Exchange or choice theory seemed to be a framework that best integrated the key elements of the diverse theories. Moreover, exchange theory also had the virtue of providing a suitable perspective to explain and answer a variety of questions and issues in the study of intimate violence, such as, Why do battered women remain with violent men?

And so, I responded to the newspaper reporter by stating,

People hit and abuse family members because *they can.*

The reporter was quite taken aback. He wanted a simple statement, but this seemed too simple. To better understand what it implies and why it is not simple at all, one has to know and appreciate some of the key assumptions of exchange theory.

Key Assumptions of Exchange Theory

An assumption of exchange theory that is relevant in explaining intimate violence is that human interaction is guided by the pursuit of rewards and the avoidance of punishment and costs. In addition, an individual who supplies reward services to another obliges him or her to fulfill an obligation, and thus the second individual must furnish benefits to the first (Blau, 1964). If reciprocal exchange of rewards occurs, the interaction will continue. But if reciprocity is not received, the interaction will be broken off.

Intrafamilial relations are more complex than those studied by traditional exchange theorists. In some instances, it is not feasible or possible to break off interaction, even if there is no reciprocity. When the "principle of distributive justice" (Blau, 1964) is violated, there can be increased anger, resent- ment, conflict, and violence.

Many students of family violence tend to view violence as the last resort to solving problems in the family. The sociologist F. Ivan Nye (1979), however, notes that this need not be the case. Spanking, for instance, is frequently the first choice of action by many parents.

When I say that people hit family members because they can, I am applying the basic assumptions of exchange theory to the case of intimate violence. People will use violence toward family members when the costs of being violent do not outweigh the rewards.

There are a variety of costs for being violent. First, there is the potential that the victim will hit back. Second, a violent assault could lead to the arrest and/or imprisonment of the person who has done the hitting. Using violence could also lead to a loss of status. Finally, too much violence might lead to the dissolution of the family or the end of the relationship. Thus, there are potential significant costs involved in being violent.

Formal and informal social control is a means of raising the costs of violent behavior. Police intervention, criminal charges, imprisonment, fines, and loss of income are all forms of formal social control that could raise the costs and lower the rewards of violent behavior. Informal social control includes loss of status, the stigma of being considered an abuser, and social ostracism—such as what O.J. Simpson experienced in the months after he was acquitted of killing his ex-wife and Ronald Goldman.

From these basic assumptions, there are certain structural properties of families that make them violence prone, and there are specific family and individual traits that make certain families more at risk for violence than other families.

Inequality, Privacy, Social Controls, and Violence

I can expand the first proposition that people hit family members because they can into three propositions:

1. Individuals are more likely to use violence in the home when they expect the costs of being violent to be less than the rewards.

2. The absence of effective social controls (e.g., police intervention) over family and intimate relations decreases the costs of one family member being violent toward another.

3. Certain social and family structures reduce social control in family relations and, therefore, reduce the costs and increase the rewards of being violent.

Inequality in the home and between men and women in general can reduce both the social control and the costs of being violent. The *private nature* of the modern family serves to reduce the degree of social control exercised over family relations (Laslett, 1973, 1978). Finally, the *image of the "real man"* in society also reduces social control in the home and intimate relations and increases the rewards of being violent.

Inequality. The normative power structure in society and the family and the resulting sexual and generational inequality in the family and intimate relations serve to reduce the chances that victims of intimate violence can threaten or inflict harm on offenders. Men are typically bigger than women, have higher-status positions, and earn more money. Because of this, they can use violence without fear of being struck back hard enough to be injured. Moreover, they do not risk having their partners take economic or social sanctions against them. Parents can use violence toward their children without fear that their children can strike back and injure them. The fact that the use of violence toward children by mothers decreases with the child's age (Gelles & Hargreaves, 1981) can be interpreted as a consequence of the greater risk of being hit back as the child grows older and larger.

Women and children may be the most frequent victims of family violence because they have no place to run and are not strong enough or do not possess sufficient resources to inflict costs on their attackers.

Privacy. Victims of family and intimate violence could turn to outside agencies to redress their grievances, but the private nature of the family and most intimate relations reduces the accessibility of outside agencies of social control. Neighbors who report that they overhear incidents of family violence also say that they fear intervening in another person's home. Police, prosecutors, and courts are often reluctant to pursue cases involving domestic violence, although this has changed in the past few years (see Chapter 7). When these cases are followed up, the courts are faced with what many judges consider the no-win position of either doing nothing or separating the combatants. Thus, to protect a child, judges may view as their only alternative to remove the child from the home. To protect the woman, the solution may be a separation or divorce. Either situation puts the legal system in the position of breaking up a family to protect the individual members. Because courts typically view this as a drastic step, such court-ordered separations or removals are comparatively rare, unless there is overwhelming or at least convincing evidence of repeated grievous injury.

Violence and the "real man." One last cost of being violent is the loss of social status that goes along with being labeled a child beater or a wife beater. However, there are subcultures where aggressive sexual and violent behavior is considered proof that someone is a "real man" (Toby, 1966). Thus, rather than risk status loss, the violent man may actually realize a status gain. Moreover, that notion that "a man's home is his castle" reduces external social control over family life.

In situations where status can be lost by being violent, individuals employ socially accepted vocabularies of motive (Mills, 1940) or "accounts" (Lyman & Scott, 1970) to explain their behavior. This process is what psychologists call rationalization. Thus, a violent father or mother might explain his or her actions by saying he or she was drunk or lost control. Parents who shared the same desire to batter their children might nod in agreement without realizing that a real loss of control would have produced a much more grievous injury or even death.

Nye (1979) developed a number of theoretical propositions using exchange theory. First, he stated,

> Violence in the family is more frequent in societies that have no legal or other normative structure prohibiting it. In societies that prohibit violence against some members (wives) but permit it against others (children), violence will be less frequent toward those members against whom it is prohibited than toward those against whom it is allowed. (p. 36)

Nye goes on to propose that wife beating and child beating are less common in families that have relatives and friends nearby, whereas child beating is more common in single-parent than in two-parent families. We would recast his propositions to read:

Family violence is more common when nonnuclear family members (e.g., friends, relatives, bystanders) are unavailable, unable, or unwilling to be part of the daily system of family interaction, and thus unable to serve as agents of formal and informal social control.

In terms of the general pattern of relationships among family members, the greater the disparity between perceived investment in a family relationship such as parenting and the perceived returns on the investment, the greater the likelihood that there will be violence. Parents who abuse teenage children (and risk being hit back) may do so because they may believe that their investment in rearing the children has yielded disappointing results.

These propositions again tend to view violence as a last resort or final alternative to an imbalance of investment and rewards in family relations. It is important to note that violence could be the first resort. Spanking children may be common because it is culturally approved and because it is immediately gratifying to the parent. Many parents justify their use of violence as a child-rearing technique because it tends to bring with it immediate emotional reward for the parent and immediate cessation of the child's offending or perceived offending behavior.

Applying Exchange/Social Control Theory

An exchange/social control theory approach to intimate violence can be extremely helpful in explaining some of the patterns of family violence that have been uncovered in empirical investigations.

The child abuse literature notes that certain types of children are at greater risk for abuse. Ill, premature, ugly, developmentally delayed, and demanding children may be at greater risk of being abused by their parents (see Chapter 3). These children either make great demands on their parents (economically, socially, or psychologically), or, as in the case of deformed children or children seen as ugly by their parents, may be perceived as not providing sufficient gratification in return for the parents' investment of time and energy. In any case, when a parent perceives the costs of parenting to outweigh the rewards, the alternatives are limited. The relationship between parent and child is difficult to break—with the exception of giving the child up for adoption or foster care, or the death of a child or parent. Thus, with few alternatives and high dissatisfaction, the parent may resort to violence or abuse.

Exchange/social control theory is also useful for explaining other findings in the study of family violence. Parents who overestimate their children's ability and capabilities may abuse them because these parents expect more out of the relationship with the children than they receive.

A similar combination of lack of alternatives and imbalance of effort invested and rewards received may be helpful in understanding other violent family relationships. Also, it is important not to lose sight of the fact that violence itself may be rewarding. Exchange theorists note that to inflict "costs" on someone who has injured you may be rewarding. The idea of "revenge being sweet" can be used to explain why wives resort to severe forms of violence in response to being punched or hit by their husbands. Also, children who assault parents who were violent, and middle-aged women who assault their elderly mothers (who may have been violent when younger), are examples of this principle of exchange theory.

In instances of violence against women, an exchange/social control theory would explain why the ending of a relationship is perhaps the most dangerous period for women (see Chapter 4). Men who are about to lose their partners and lose control of the relationship may feel the costs of the relationship ending and the costs of losing control of their partners may outweigh whatever costs might be associated with beating their partners. The end of the relationship and the loss of control may change the calculus of costs and rewards for some men.

Research on the effect of mandatory arrest policies also suggests that the balance of costs and rewards might influence the use and escalation of violence toward women. Criminologist Lawrence Sherman (1992) examined the results from six studies that examined the effectiveness of mandatory arrest policies (see Chapter 7). Sherman reports that arrest had different effects depending on who was arrested. Men who were employed and who were married to the women they assaulted were less likely to be violent against them after they were arrested. On the other hand, men who were not married to the women they assaulted and who were not employed were actually more violent toward their partners after being arrested for minor (misdemeanor level) violent assaults. Sherman explains that men with a greater stake in conforming to conventional society were more likely to be deterred by the formal social control of arrest, whereas men with less stake in conformity were actually made more violent by the arrest, perhaps using violence against their partners to rebel against formal social control. From an exchange/social control perspective, the less men had to lose by being violent (the lower the costs to them of being arrested), the more violent they would and could be. On the other hand, the more men had to lose by being arrested and publicly identified as a wife beater, the less likely they would be violent again.

The sociologist Kirk Williams (1992) tested the propositions of exchange/social control theory of family violence using data from the Second National Family Violence Survey and follow-up studies carried out the next 2 years (1986 and 1987). The findings from the study suggested that men who believed themselves more isolated from the police (greater privacy), who were more powerful in their relationship with their partners (greater inequality), and who approved of men hitting their partners were less likely to consider being arrested as costly to them. Those men who perceived the costs of arrest low were more likely to assault their partners. Thus, there is some empirical support of the main propositions of exchange/social control theory.

Toward Preventing and Treating Intimate Violence

One of the virtues of an exchange/social control theory of intimate violence is that it has direct applications to the prevention and treatment of intimate violence. Again, to oversimplify, if violence occurs in intimate relations because people *can* be violent, then the goal of prevention and treatment is to make it so they cannot. To do this requires practitioners and social policy planners to consider how they can increase the degree of social control over families, raise the costs of violence, and reduce the rewards. The final chapter of this text considers programs and policies that are designed to treat violent families as well as preventing violence before it can occur.

DISCUSSION QUESTIONS

1. How does the private nature of the family contribute to both love and violence within families?

2. What are some of the "rewards" of being violent in families?

SUGGESTED ASSIGNMENTS

1. Design model legislation for either child abuse or wife abuse that would raise the costs of violence in families.

2. Assume that you have been asked to testify before a state legislature or Congress on the topic of preventing family violence. Based on the theories that attempt to explain family violence, what would you recommend? Prepare your testimony.

7

PREVENTION AND TREATMENT

Society's Response and Responsibility

I f people are violent and abusive toward family members and intimate partners because they can be, because the advantages outweigh the costs, and because the privacy of intimate relations decreases social control, then how do we break the cycle of violence? How do we protect victims of violence? More important, how can we prevent violence from occurring? I concluded the previous chapter by stating that the goal of prevention and treatment is to make it so people cannot be violent. But what does this mean? What programs and policies will make it so people cannot be violent? What should we do?

Initially, the response to intimate violence was to assume that abusive individuals were mentally ill. But over the past three decades, the tendency to diagnose the causes of violence as a psychological abnormality or mental illness has declined. We realize now that individual psychiatric care for violent offenders is but one limited treatment for the problem. Because the roots of intimate violence lie in the structure of the family, intimate relations, and society, we know that individual psychiatric treatment can be effective with only a small number of cases of violence and abuse. Individual and family counseling are still important steps in intervening in intimate violence, but a variety of programs and policies have been developed that deal with other structural sources of violence.

One of the roadblocks to effective treatment of intimate violence is the fact that child abuse and domestic violence were recognized and treated by completely separate institutions and systems. There is little, if any, overlap in the treatment programs aimed at either child or woman abuse. There is little recognition of the problem of relationship, intimate, or family violence. Each group identifies its own problems, develops its own treatment, secures its own funds, and in an era of scarce money for social services, jealously guards its own turf. One of the notable gaps in the entire treatment program is a recognition of the problem of intimate violence and the development of treatment modalities for the entire range of the problem.

I begin this chapter by reviewing the steps that have been taken to aid in discovering private violence. Over the past three decades, laws have been passed and policies have been implemented by the criminal justice and social welfare systems to help recognize and identify various forms of intimate violence. But recognition and identification of violence and abuse is but the first step in treating and preventing violence and abuse. Intervention, once an instance of violence is publicly identified, poses an important problem. Should we respond with efforts to *control* violence, or should our approach be one of *compassion* for the offender as well as the victim? I examine the dilemma of compassion versus control in the next section. The section following reviews the various treatment programs that have been developed to deal with various types of intimate violence. Finally, the chapter concludes with a discussion of prevention, and I present a number of important steps that should be taken if we want to reduce the tragic toll of intimate violence in society.

From Behind Closed Doors: Recognizing Intimate Violence

Child Abuse: Reporting Laws

Because violence was hidden behind the closed doors of American households for so many years, one of the initial policy approaches was to make sure that abuse and violence were recognized publicly so that human service professionals could respond with the proper treatment. In the first decade after child abuse was recognizeo as a significant health and social problem, a great amount of effort went into assuring that abused children would be identified. Between 1962 and 1967, all 50 states and the District of Columbia enacted mandatory child abuse reporting laws that required designated professionals to report suspected cases of child abuse. Mandatory reporting laws were designed to bring child abuse out from behind closed doors. There are many professionals who see children daily and who see the visible and emotional signs of abuse and neglect. However, prior to the enactment of reporting laws, many professionals, including physicians and teachers, were extremely reluctant to report cases of child abuse. The reasons for failing to report were many and varied. Some professionals were unaware of the signs of abuse and often accepted the explanation that the bruises and scars were the results of accidents. Even if the signs of abuse were clearly identifiable (e.g., a hand mark on the side of the face), professionals were still reluctant to become involved in what most people considered to be a "family matter." Fear of being sued for false accusation also played a part in failure to report. Last, professionals and the public alike frequently did not know to whom to report cases of abuse.

Gradually, state laws were drafted that mandated specific professionals (or in some states, all adults) to report suspected abuse. To protect people who made reports in good faith, state statutes provided that people making reports in good faith could not be sued for false accusation. When it appeared that the early versions of the law still were not generating adequate numbers of reports, some states added criminal penalties for failing to report cases of suspected abuse. In addition to passing laws, states also engaged in public awareness campaigns and public education programs. The initial effect of such campaigns was startling. Florida began one of the first public awareness programs in the early 1970s. Along with the program, Florida provided a toll-free number for people to call and report suspected cases of abuse. Reports of child abuse in Florida before the public awareness campaign were less than 20 per year. In the first year after the campaign (1971), there were 19,000 reports of suspected abuse!

As I pointed out in Chapter 3, reports of suspected child maltreatment have increased substantially since states enacted mandatory reporting laws. Reports increased 332% between 1976 and 1993 (U.S. Department of Health and Human Services, National Center on Child Abuse and Neglect, 1995). Not all reports that are made are substantiated or determined to be valid after investigation. There were 2,935,470 individual children reported for suspected abuse and neglect in 1994. As a result of these reports, state agencies conducted about 1.63 million investigations. Overall, 38.1% of the children reported were either substantiated or indicated as abused or neglected.[1] An estimated 6% of the unsubstantiated charges were deliberate false reports (U.S. Department of Health and Human Services, National Center on Child Abuse and Neglect, 1996). According to the National Committee to Prevent Child Abuse, the rate of substantiated child abuse reports has declined from 36% in 1991 to 33% in 1994 (Weise & Daro, 1995). That 6 out of 10 reports are not substantiated has led some observers to state that they believe child abuse is overreported, and state agencies have a difficult time protecting abused children because they spend so much time investigating unsubstantiated, or what some call "false," reports (Besharov, 1993; Wexler, 1991).

On the other hand, child welfare experts know that not every suspected case of child maltreatment is reported. Gail Zellman (1990a, 1990b) surveyed 1,200 mandated reporters. More than half of those mandated to report child maltreatment had reported a case in the prior year. However, 40% of the mandated reporters said that they had, at some time in their professional careers, failed to report a suspected case of child abuse and neglect. More than 1 in 5 (22%) said they had failed to report a case of abuse just in the year prior to the survey. There were a number of reasons why a mandated reporter would ignore the law and fail to report a case. The reason most cited in Zellman's survey was the professional's belief that the evidence was not sufficient to warrant a report (even though the law requires *suspected*, but not proven, cases be reported). Another reason was that professionals believed that they could do more to help the child and family than the child protection agency could. A number of nonreporting professionals said that child protection workers overreact to reports, that all their services are of poor quality, or both. A smaller portion of professionals explained that they failed to report because reporting would be bad for them because making the report took too much time, they would have to leave work to testify in court, or they would feel uncomfortable dealing with the family in the future if they filed a child abuse report. Some professionals said they did not even know how to make a report or would not make one because it would breach confidentiality (even though the law allows such a breach in instances of suspected child abuse). Thus, there are those in the field of child maltreatment who believe that child abuse is still underreported and that mandatory reporting laws and public education campaigns still need to be supported (Finkelhor, 1993).

Violence Against Women: Criminalization

Battered wives are treated differently than abused children. Because most people assume that adult women are capable of reporting their own victimization, there have been no calls for implementing reporting laws for battered women, although one state, California, does have a mandatory reporting law for spouse abuse, and other states require physicians to report intentional injuries. Yet women still have the problem of being victimized behind closed doors. If the shame and stigma of being a battered wife was not bad enough, many state laws actually stipulated that for a wife to charge her husband with assault and battery, she had to be more severely injured than someone who was assaulted by a stranger.

The criminal justice system, beginning with the role and actions of the police, traditionally approached wife abuse from various perspectives —denial, acceptance, lack of awareness, and helplessness. Some police departments used "stitch rules" to respond to cases of domestic assault—a wife who was abused had to require a certain number of surgical sutures before a husband would be arrested for assault and battery (Field & Field, 1973). Prosecutors frequently failed to take the complaints of battered women seriously and sent women home with the advice that they should "kiss and make up."

Many law enforcement officials who try to assist battered wives complain that the wives themselves handcuff the criminal justice system. Police frequently claim that women attack and even kill police officers who are called on to intervene in domestic violence. Other police officers point to the numerous instances where women who have been beaten fail to file charges against their husbands or withdraw the charges within a few days of the violent episode. Some prosecutors also explain that women frequently fail to follow through in pressing charges. Some women have actually dropped charges at the trial, and one announced that "husbands are supposed to hit their wives, aren't they?" (Parnas, 1967).

Statements such as the one that claims that husbands are supposed to hit their wives created a kind of self-fulfilling prophecy in which people and prosecutors expected that all battered women would fail to follow through with legal actions. Consequently, police and prosecutors often advised victims against taking legal action. As a result, police and district attor- neys were seen as less than sympathetic to the problem of battered women. Organized women's groups spent much of the 1970s seeking equal protection for battered women. Class action suits were filed to assure that police and prosecutors paid attention to the problem of battered women. In December 1976, women in New York City filed a class action suit against the New York Police Department, probation officers, and family court employees for failing to prosecute abusive husbands. The police settled out of court in 1977. In 1974, a class action suit was filed against the Cleveland district attorneys for denying battered women equal protec- tion under the law by not following through in prosecution of abusive husbands. That suit was settled by a consent decree ordering prosecutors to change their practices. In Oakland, California, the police were accused of illegal conduct because of their pattern and practice of discouraging arrests in cases of domestic violence. In all these class action suits, the central goal was to eliminate the selective inattention to the problem of battered women and to criminalize violence against women.

Perhaps the most influential lawsuit was the one filed by Tracy Thurman (*Thurman v. City of Torrington*, 595 F. Supp. 1521, 1984). Thurman was a battered wife who had frequently sought help from the Torrington, Connecticut, police because of the violent attacks of her estranged husband. Thurman was badly battered and left permanently injured in June 1983 and subsequently filed suit against the city of Torrington and 29 police officers. Thurman was initially awarded $2.3 million and later settled out of court for $1.9 million. The threat of similar suits motivated a number of cities in the northeast to adopt mandatory arrest policies in cases of spouse abuse. The case received national attention when it was turned into a made-for-television movie, "A Cry for Help."

At the beginning of the 1970s, few states had laws aimed at reducing spousal violence. Today, all states have enacted legislation on domestic violence. Most of the state laws created new civil and criminal legal remedies for persons abused by family or household members. Some state laws specify the powers and duties of the police and courts in handling domestic violence. Some laws mandate social agencies to provide services to violent families. Finally, a number of states have enacted laws that provide funding for battered woman shelters. As pointed out in Chapter 4, the federal government enacted the Violence Against Women Act in 1994. This act not only provides funds for programs and services, but it also allows for federal prosecution of crimes "motivated by gender" against women and makes it a federal crime to travel across state lines to violate a protective order.

Siblings, Adolescents, and
Elders: Few Legal Remedies

In general, the legal remedies applied to child abuse and spousal violence have not been specifically aimed at what I referred to in Chapter 5 as the hidden victims of family violence. Adolescent victims of violence are technically covered by child abuse statutes, but as we saw in Chapter 5, adolescents are rarely reported as victims of physical child abuse. Sibling violence is covered only by normal laws pertaining to criminal assault. This too is the case for violence toward parents. The only exception to this pattern is that 42 states have enacted reporting laws aimed at victims of elder abuse.

Intervention in Intimate Violence:
Compassion or Control

Once a case of intimate violence is reported or recognized, the next important step is to intervene. What should be done? As I have noted numerous times in this book, the first emotional reaction to child abuse is to call for stiff and harsh penalties to be meted out against abusive parents. In addition to punishing parents, people frequently advise that the children should be taken away from abusive parents. Similarly, removal of elderly victims of abuse from the homes of their abusers is considered an important first step in treating elder abuse.

The physicians Alvin Rosenfeld and Eli Newberger (1977) have noted two competing philosophies that have been applied to treating child abuse. These philosophies are equally applicable to other forms of intimate violence intervention.

On the one hand is the compassionate approach. Human service professionals who treat violence and abuse from this perspective approach it with an abundance of human kindness and a nonpunitive outlook on intervention. The compassionate philosophy views the abusers as victims themselves. The cause of the abuse may be seen in social and developmental origins, and not in the abuser. Abusers, rather than being seen as cold, cruel monsters, are seen as sad, deprived, and needy human beings. Compassionate intervention involves supporting the abuser and his or her family. Homemaker services, health and child care, counseling, and other supports are made available to the family.

On the other hand is the control model. The control model involves aggressive use of intervention to limit and, if necessary, punish the deviant violent behavior. The control approach places full responsibility for actions with the abuser. Control involves removal of the child from the home, arrest of an abusive husband (or wife), and full criminal prosecution of the offender.

The compassion model has dangers for the clinician and the family. The compassionate clinician may strive to support a family and may actually raise the risk of further violence by relieving the offender from responsibility. A clinician's concern for alienating abusive parents or abusive partners may compromise the clinician's judgment and result in a victim being left at risk. In addition, should the compassionate approach fail to result in positive change, the human service professional may be left feeling demoralized and burned out.

Human service professionals are reluctant to use the control approach, even when the situation literally screams out for action. Clinicians have been heard to say that they were reluctant to use stern measures because "the family has already suffered enough." Sadly, on some occasions, a control approach may actually raise the risks for abused children and women. On one occasion in the state of Rhode Island, a child was removed from a mother who was neglecting the child. The child was placed in a foster home, only to be beaten to death 6 months later by the foster father. When women flee battering relationships for shelter, this can enrage the husband to the point of homicide, as happened to a woman in Boston who was attacked and killed by her husband a few blocks from the shelter.

There is no easy solution to the control/compassion dilemma. Rosenfeld and Newberger (1977) call for giving compassion *and* control. Assessment and intervention functions should probably be performed by separate individuals. A control approach might be used in assessment, while compassion is reserved for use once the proper course of treatment is prescribed for the family. In the best of all possible worlds, the choice of intervention would not boil down to a choice between protecting the child or woman by removal versus keeping the family together. The best of all possible worlds would involve appropriate measures of legal control and humane support. The following section reviews the standard and useful forms of treatment that have been developed for dealing with intimate violence.

Treatment

As we saw in the previous section, any program or policy designed to treat the problem of intimate violence must be capable of protecting the victim(s) while preventing further violence—if possible by strengthening the family. Without both of these components, there is no long-term solution to violence in the home.

Treating Child Abuse

Identification and reporting. The first step in treating child abuse is to identify children in need of services. Consequently, considerable effort has been devoted to improving techniques of identifying and reporting cases of child abuse to the proper human service agencies. Such steps involve a variety of efforts, which are coordinated among numerous public and private agencies. First, as I already mentioned, all 50 states enacted legislation that required reporting suspected cases of child maltreatment. To assure that cases would and could be properly identified, public and private agencies engaged in training programs to educate potential reporters about the signs of abuse. These public education and awareness programs greatly increased the number of child abuse and neglect reports that were generated. Because of this, states and localities established child abuse hot lines that were staffed 24 hours per day. These hot lines were designed to receive reports. Soon states found that they also required 24-hour-a-day response capabilities.

Child welfare services: Preserve and protect. It should be obvious from the discussion of the incidence of child abuse in Chapter 3 that if all cases of child abuse and violence toward children were reported to public and private social welfare agencies, and if each reported case was fully investigated and provided services, it would tax the existing social welfare system beyond its present means. In many if not most states, child welfare or protective service workers are already burdened with caseloads that are far too large to allow the workers to service the child and family adequately—and this is when people estimate that only one of three child abuse cases is being reported! Some caseworkers have caseloads of 30 and even 50 families, whereas most professionals in the field of social and human services believe that protective workers should serve no more than 20 families at a time.

The optimal situation for child welfare agencies is to be able to respond to problems of child abuse quickly, effectively, and in a manner that treats the causes of abuse, not just the symptoms. Child welfare systems need to be able to provide immediate crisis intervention when children are at risk. Ideally, a protective service system ought to be able to respond to all reports of child abuse and neglect and be able to supply emergency resources for the child and family immediately, or at least within 24 hours of the report.

The nature of the child welfare response is even more important than how fast response can be made. Professionals in the field of child protection recommend that child welfare agencies be able to provide emergency homemaker services, a hot line to help parents deal with day-to-day crises, transportation, child care services, counseling or referrals for professional counseling, health care, clothing and shelter, access to self-help groups such as Parents Anonymous, and other resources that ease the burden of child care for parents.

Finding the proper balance between compassion and control has been a major challenge for the child welfare system. Mandatory reporting, thorough and rapid investigation of child abuse reports, and removing abused and neglected children from abusive parents and placing the children in foster care represent the control side of child welfare services. Intensive casework services, plans to find permanent placements for children, and using foster care as a last resort constitute the compassionate side of the system. Some observers see the attempt to find a balance between these two approaches as a pendulum that swings from control to compassion and back, depending on current theories about the causes of maltreatment, the development of new interventions, and publicity around sensational cases (Lindsey, 1994). The case of the Rhode Island boy who was killed in foster care received widespread media coverage and led to the system reducing the number of maltreatment children placed into foster care. Sensational child homicides, such as Joseph Wallace in Chicago in 1993 or Elisa Izquierdo in New York in December 1995, caused the pendulum to swing back to the control side and prompted calls for children to be removed from abusive caretakers.

Although child welfare policy does tend to swing back and forth like a pendulum between compassion and control, the essential philosophy of the child welfare system is one of compassion. Ideally, the system aims at supporting and preserving families as a means of protecting children from maltreatment.

Family preservation programs are not new. They go back at least to the settlement house movement created at Hull House in Chicago by Jane Addams in 1910. Family preservation programs are designed to help children and families (including extended and adoptive families) that are at risk or in crisis.

Although family preservation programs have been a key component of the child welfare system for nearly a century, the rediscovery of child abuse and neglect in the early 1960s and the conceptualization of the problem as one arising out of the psychopathology of the parents or caretakers changed the child welfare emphasis from one of preserving families to one of protecting children. With the implementation of mandatory reporting laws and the resulting dramatic increase in child abuse and neglect reports, child welfare agencies turned more often to removal of children from homes deemed at risk. Maltreated children were placed in temporary placements—typically foster homes. By 1978, it was estimated that there were some 500,000 children in foster care in the United States (Pelton, 1989; Tatara, 1993a).

By the end of the 1970s, there was increasing concern about the number of children in foster care and the cost. In addition, the model of child abuse that explained abuse as a result of individual personality disorder or mental illness had been replaced by explanations of maltreatment that emphasized social factors, such as poverty, stress, social isolation, and lack of understanding of proper parenting skills (see Chapter 6).

Thus, there was widespread questioning of both the need to remove so many children from their biological homes and the effectiveness of foster care as a means of dealing with child maltreatment. Researchers and practitioners assumed that the funds spent on foster care could be more effectively used supporting and preserving families.

Intensive family preservation programs were developed as a means of protecting children and preserving families. In 1974, David Haapala and Jill Kinney were husband and wife and child psychologists who, with a group of social workers, submitted a grant application to the National Institute of Mental Health (NIMH) for funding for a "super foster home." The proposal called for a facility that would help foster parents in Tacoma, Washington, cope with "out of control" adolescents. Jack Bartleson, the contact person at the NIMH, suggested a counterproposal—why not work with families *before* a child is removed. Instead of putting resources into foster care, why not apply resources to try to keep the original birth family together? More important, Bartleson suggested, why not provide the services in the home—have the social workers actually move in with the family? (Barthel, 1991).

Haapala and Kinney labeled their program "Homebuilders." Homebuilders became the model of intensive family preservation services. The goal of Homebuilders and all intensive family preservation programs is to safely maintain children in their homes or to facilitate a safe and lasting reunification. Homebuilders services are supposed to be limited to families where there is a serious crisis threatening the stability of the family and the safety of family members, or where reunification is being pursued after a maltreated child has been placed outside of the home.

The essential feature is that family preservation services are intensive, short-term, crisis interventions. Services are provided in the client's home, although social workers do not actually move in. The length of home visit is variable—it is not confined to the "50-minute" clinical hour. Services are available 7 days a week, 24 hours a day, not just during business hours Monday through Friday. Caseloads are small—two or three families per worker. Soft services, such as therapy and education, and hard services, such as food stamps, housing, a homemaker, and supplemental Social Security, are available. But the most important difference between Homebuilders and traditional family reunification programs is the intensive, short-term nature of the program. Although services can be provided daily, Homebuilders was designed to be short term. Finally, whereas traditional child welfare programs are based on a deficit model that assumes that abusive parents do not have the personal, social, or economic resources to cope with raising children, intensive family preservation programs are designed to identify and work with families around their strengths. Thus, if a family has a strong network of relatives, the work focuses on using this network to help with family stressors or crises.

The initial evaluations of intensive family preservation programs were uniformly enthusiastic. The programs were claimed to have reduced the placement of children while assuring the safety of those children. Foundation program officers and program administrators claimed that the families involved in intensive family preservation programs had low rates of placement and "100% safety records" (Barthel, 1991; Forsythe, 1992).

There were, however, major methodological problems with the early evaluations of intensive family preservation programs, including the fact that most of the evaluations did not use control groups and those that did failed to use appropriately matched control groups (the control groups were not similar in terms of type of maltreatment and social characteristics to the groups receiving intensive family preservation services). In his 1992 review, sociologist Peter Rossi concluded that evaluation studies he reviewed did not demonstrate that intensive family preservation programs reduced placement or reduced child welfare program costs.

To date, no evaluation study that uses a randomly assigned control group has found that intensive family preservation programs reduce placement, costs, or the risk of maltreatment (Gelles, 1996; Heneghan, Horwitz, & Leventhal, 1996; Lindsey, 1994; Schuerman, Rzepnicki, & Littell, 1994).

Thus, the empirical case for intensive family preservation has not been made. Moreover, there are many critics of family preservation, such as myself (Gelles, 1996), who argue that the belief that intensive family preservation programs are effective and the emphasis on keeping children with abusive parents or reuniting children with parents after the parents have had intensive services actually places many children at risk of re-abuse or even fatal abuse.

The debate between compassion and control continues. Critics of the child welfare system propose that cases of serious abuse should become the responsibility of the police, who are better equipped to investigate and intervene in serious cases of physical abuse, sexual abuse, and neglect (Lindsey, 1994). Others argue that the child welfare system should provide more in the way of real social work instead of merely investigating reports and removing children from their homes (Hagedorn, 1995). My own preference would be to abandon the belief that one intervention, like

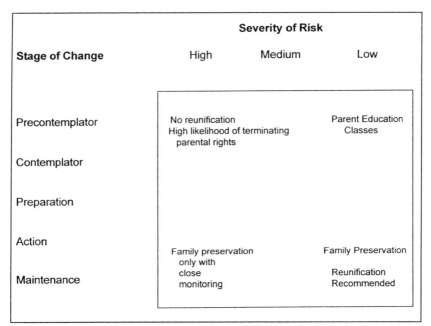

Figure 7.1. Two Dimensions of Risk Assessment for Child Abuse and Neglect
SOURCE: R. J. Gelles (1996), *The Book of David: How Preserving Families Can Cost Children's Lives*, © 1996, Basic Books, New York. Used with permission.

intensive family preservation programs, can be effective for all families. Some families cannot be preserved, and others should not be preserved. Rather than arguing that the pendulum should swing one way or another, my position is that interventions should be *targeted* for families depending on the severity of abuse, the age of the child, the level of risk for future abuse, and the readiness of the parents or caretakers to actually change. Figure 7.1 illustrates a method of targeting interventions depending on risk and readiness to change, based on a model of change developed by James Prochaska and his colleagues (Prochaska, Norcross, & DiClemente, 1994).

Treating Violence Against Women

Intervening in instances of violence against women involves different services and different institutions than those that are used to ameliorate the problem of child maltreatment. Here again, however, there is a tension between compassionate and control approaches. There is no question that victims of violence against women require a compassionate approach that includes providing for the victim's present and future safety as well as empowering the victim to help her live free of violence in the future. Treatment approaches for men, on the other hand, pit counseling and treatment approaches against the use of arrest, prosecution, and criminal justice sanctions.

Because the victims are adults, conventional wisdom leads one to assume that they are able to take care of themselves and are not helpless victims of violence. There are only a few mandatory reporting laws for wife abuse. Few agencies even bother to keep records of cases of wife abuse or violence against women. Police records note wife abuse either as "domestic disturbances" or, rarely, as "assault." Hospitals rarely separate cases of wife assault or violence against women by male partners from other emergency cases. There are some adult protective units in social service agencies, but they typically focus their attention on dependent or vulnerable adults—for instance, elderly victims.

The main crisis intervention services that victims of abuse can turn to are the police, courts, and battered woman shelters.

The police. Family disturbance calls have been labeled the "common cold" of police work (Elliott, 1989). These calls, many of which involve violence between spouses, constitute the largest single category of calls received by police departments each year (Police Foundation, 1977). The American police officer frequently functions as the neighborhood social worker. In cases of child abuse, police are often called on to intervene in ongoing instances of violence or neglect of children, and their primary function in these instances is to report the abuse or neglect to the proper child welfare authorities. But in cases of domestic violence, the police not only are the first on the scene of ongoing violence, but they also are the agents of social control who command the primary power to protect the victims.

Sociologists Sarah Berk and Donileen Loseke (1980) note that "as front-line agents of social control in domestic disturbances, police are the proximate representative of state policy" (p. 318). The alternative social services that are available to women, such as shelters, most often depend on the police for cooperation; police must inform domestic violence victims of the availability of these services. The police are a crucial link between the victim and treatment programs available in her community.

Police intervention into cases of domestic violence can be dangerous work, and some police officers have been injured or killed during attempts to intervene in domestic disturbance calls. Domestic disturbance calls are among the least glamorous and least prestigious tasks in which officers engage. Few officers receive medals or promotions because they are effective in handling domestic violence calls.

Because domestic violence calls can be extremely dangerous and the rewards are few, police were rarely motivated to get involved in treatment or prevention. In the 1970s, family violence professionals were quite critical of the then traditional police reluctance to intervene and ameliorate family violence (Dobash & Dobash, 1979; Field & Field, 1973).

Berk and Loseke (1980) studied the factors that influenced police officers' decisions about how to intervene in domestic assault. Examining data from 262 official police reports concerning domestic disturbances in Santa Barbara, California, Berk and Loseke found four factors that were related to whether police decided to arrest a violent husband. If the wife-victim signed an arrest warrant, if both husband and wife were present when the police arrived, if the wife alleged that violence had occurred, or if the husband was drunk when the police arrived, the likelihood that an arrest would be made increased. However, if the wife made the original call to the police, this actually reduced the chances that the husband would be arrested. Thus, the traditional complaint that police do not effectively intervene because they, as an occupational group, support the right of husbands to hit their wives, and the complaint that the police are reluctant to get involved in "family matters" do not seem to hold under analysis. The data suggest that situational factors, not occupational attitudes, affect police decision making.

In the past few years, the treatment of choice for the criminal justice "common cold" has changed from apparent indifference or compassionate mediation to firmer control and mandatory or "presumptive" arrest. A number of factors have led to a wide-scale adoption of control strategies for dealing with domestic violence and more specifically, violence toward women. One important factor was the feminist and women's movement argument that the criminal justice system was indifferent to violence against women. Those advancing this argument claimed that the criminal justice system, and especially the police, treated domestic violence differently than instances of stranger assault. Feminist critics asserted that the police assign domestic disturbance calls a low priority, do not respond or delay response to these categories of calls, and avoid arrest or use of other control strategies in favor of simply restoring order or calming the violent parties down.

A second major factor that moved police departments toward a control approach and adoption of mandatory or presumptive arrest strategies was the publication of the results of the Minneapolis Police Experiment (Sherman & Berk, 1984). This study, funded by the National Institute of Justice and conducted by the Police Foundation, called for the police in two precincts in Minneapolis to randomly assign violent family offenders to one of three experimental conditions: arrest, separation, or advice/ mediation. Eligible households were those in which both offender and victim were present when the police arrived and the nature of the incident was classified as "misdemeanor assault." A 6-month period followed the experimental condition during which interviews were conducted with victims and offenders. Official reports of subsequent incidents of family violence were also collected. An analysis of the follow-up data indicated that those receiving the arrest intervention had the lowest rate of recidivism (10%) and those who were separated had the highest (24%). Advice and mediation cases had a 19% recidivism rate.

The public announcement in April 1983 and subsequent publication of the results of the Minneapolis Police Experiment led a number of large urban police departments to adopt mandatory or presumptive arrest interventions in cases of domestic assault. By January 1987, 176 cities across the United States were using some form of arrest policy.

A third factor that led to the adoption of arrest strategies was the publication of the U.S. Attorney General's Task Force on Family Violence report (U.S. Department of Justice, 1984). Drawing heavily from the results of the Minneapolis Police Experiment, this report called for police departments and criminal justice agencies to recognize family violence as criminal activity and respond accordingly. The report recommended arrest as the preferred strategy for responding to cases of family violence.

A fourth factor may have been the case of *Thurman v. the City of Torrington*, discussed earlier in this chapter. The firmer control approach to domestic violence, however, was not as effective as the initial results of the Minneapolis Police Experiment suggested it might be. Subsequent to the publication of the results of the Minneapolis Police Experiment, the National Institute of Justice funded six replications of the experiment. Researchers examined the effectiveness of mandatory arrest in Atlanta,

Georgia; Charlotte, North Carolina; Colorado Springs, Colorado; Milwaukee, Wisconsin; and Miami, Florida (Berk, Campbell, Klap, & Western, 1992; Dunford, Huizinga, & Elliott, 1990; Hirschell, Hutchinson, & Dean, 1990; Pate & Hamilton, 1992; Sherman & Smith, 1992). Contrary to the evidence from Minneapolis, the major findings from five of the replications (no data were reported from the study in Atlanta) was that arrest, and the immediate period of custody associated with arrest, was not a deterrent to continued violence.

Although arrest, in and of itself, did not appear to put victims at greater danger of continued violence compared to separation or mediation, there were results from the studies that did indicate under what circumstances arrest might be effective and might create danger for women. Sherman (1992) found that men who were married to the women they assaulted and who were employed were less likely to be violent again after being arrested. However, men who were not married to their victims and who were unemployed reduced their use of violence for a short period of time and then actually were more violent than they had been prior to their arrest. Sherman explains that "stake in conformity" explained the deterrent effect of arrest for married and employed men. The more men had to lose, the more they were deterred by arrest. For men who had little to lose, an arrest actually enraged them and caused them to retaliate against their partners.

A second finding from the series of arrest studies supported the deterrent effect of the *threat* of legal sanctions. If the offender was not present when the police arrived and an arrest warrant was issued, these men were deterred from engaging in future violence (Dunford et al., 1990). This result supports the efficacy of the threat of legal sanctions, even though actual arrest seems to do little to reduce subsequent domestic violence.

Although arrest may have a deterrent effect only for certain types of offenders, this does not mean that control interventions are of no use in treating and preventing violence against women. Most of the offenders who are arrested are not prosecuted once they are arrested. Second, the studies of the deterrent effects of arrest examined only cases of misdemeanor violence. Thus, it is possible that arrest combined with sanctions and arrest of felony offenders may reduce the occurrence of domestic assault.

The courts. The second line of defense for victims of domestic violence is the court system. Court-imposed intervention includes the issuance of protective orders or restraining orders to keep violent men out of the home and away from their partners and children. Peace bonds can be imposed along with these orders to add the deterrent effect of lost money should the order be violated. Prosecution for less than lethal family violence is still problematic, and some prosecutors and judges still retain vestiges of viewing domestic violence as a family matter.

Only a tiny fraction of incidents of marital violence reach a courtroom. In a national survey of family violence (Gelles & Straus, 1988), more than 800 homes reported some form of marital violence in the preceding year. Only five of these cases (about one half of 1%) went to court. This number constitutes a mere 13% of those cases of violence in which the police were called. The few cases of spouse assault that ended up in court resulted in a variety of actions. These actions included dismissing the charges, warning the abuser, requiring the abuser to enter counseling, fining the abuser, jail, or a suspended sentence. Respondents indicated a wide ranging levels of satisfaction with the results of their appearances in court. Thirty percent were very satisfied, 7% were somewhat satisfied, 20% were somewhat dissatisfied, and nearly 8% were very dissatisfied. The largest percentage, more than one third, said they were not sure. One means of improving the effectiveness of prosecution of domestic violence has been the creation of special prosecution units. Special domestic violence prosecution units increase incentives for vigorous prosecution of domestic violence. In addition, some prosecutors have adopted "no-drop policies" that do not allow women to drop charges before or even during a trial. Although no-drop policies do reduce frustration faced by police and prosecutors, they also reduce the control women have over their own cases and desires and may discourage women from using the legal system. David Ford (1991) explains that no-drop policies or mandatory prosecution may work against empowering women.

Also, special domestic violence courts have been created for spouse and partner assault cases. Special courts are designed to resolve the problem of domestic violence cases receiving lower priority for prosecution in the judicial system and to allow the court to combine criminal prosecution with counseling or treatment programs under judicial oversight.

One of the most widely used forms of criminal justice intervention has been the protective or restraining order. Such orders may require the defendant to do one of several things: desist from abuse, refrain from contacting the plaintiff, vacate or stay away from the plaintiff's residence or place of work, surrender custody of minor children, pay child support, or otherwise compensate for financial losses (Isaac, Cochran, Brown, & Adams, 1994). Temporary protective or restraining orders may be issued *ex parte*, that is, they may be issued to women without the necessity of having her partner appear before the judge or magistrate.

Over the years, the process of seeking and receiving restraining or protective orders has been streamlined and simplified. Thus, there has been a tremendous growth in the number of women seeking such orders and judges granting them. For instance, more than 50,000 restraining orders were issued in Massachusetts between September 1992 and September 1993 (Isaac et al., 1994).

To date, there has been no actual evaluation of the effectiveness of restraining and protective orders. There is no evidence that such orders actually deter men from contacting or abusing their partners, and there is at least anecdotal evidence that in some cases, such orders may actually do more harm than good. As with other criminal justice interventions, the problem with restraining and protective orders is that they have few teeth and thus fail to deter determined batterers.

Shelters. Perhaps the most important development in the past 20 years in treating domestic violence has been the grassroots development of battered woman shelters or safe houses. One of the first shelters designed to protect victims of intimate violence was created almost by accident. As I mentioned in Chapter 2, in 1971 a group of women in Chiswick, England, met to discuss rising food prices. But prices were not their biggest complaint—loneliness was. Out of these first meetings a Women's Aid project was established by Erin Pizzey. Soon a house was set up as Chiswick Women's Aid. The house became a center for women with personal problems. Before long, the house filled up with women with a common problem—abuse. Within 3 years, Women's Aid of Chiswick became the model for women's shelters around the world.

In 1976, there were probably no more than five or six shelters in the United States. By 1996, there were approximately 1,800 programs for victims of domestic violence, of which 1,200 were shelters for battered women. Some shelters actually are the result of class projects organized by students enrolled in family violence courses at colleges and universities.

Shelters were initially designed to provide refuge or safety for victims of domestic violence. Today, shelters and programs provide a variety of services, including hot lines, temporary shelter services, support groups, group and individual counseling, legal advocacy, social service referral and advocacy, services for children of abused women, transitional housing, child care, and job training. The shelter movement has been at the center of public education and public awareness campaigns designed to change social attitudes and advocate for needed legal and institutional changes to prevent violence against women. Thus, shelters and shelter-based programs provide short-term crisis intervention and long-term social support for victims of intimate violence.

Shelters have various capabilities, abilities, and rules. Some can hold 30 women; some can hold only a few. Most women seem to stay for a week or two before they leave. Researchers report that anywhere from one third to two thirds of the women who come to shelters do not return to their violent mates (Giles-Sims, 1983; Sedlak, 1988).

Although shelters are a major source of intervention for victims of domestic violence, we have little data on the number of women who desire shelter services or the characteristics of clients of shelters. Most of those involved with providing services for battered women believe that there is insufficient shelter space for women, and battered women are often turned away because of lack of space. The women who do seek or stay at a shelter tend to be from lower socioeconomic groups. Christine O'Sullivan and her colleagues (O'Sullivan, Wise, & Douglass, 1995) found that more than three fourths of the women who sought shelter were on public assistance. Obviously, women with more economic resources may find shelter at a hotel or motel, may have the money to take a plane to stay with a friend or relative in another city, or may seek help from private sources, such as a lawyer or counselor.

There has been a handful of studies on the effect of shelters. Andrea Sedlak (1988) reports that women who stayed in shelters for nontrivial periods of time (3 weeks) evidenced decreases in depression and increased independence from their abusers. Sociologist Jean Giles-Sims (1983) studied 31 women who sought help from a shelter. She interviewed 24 of these women 6 months after they left the shelter and found that the shelter had beneficial effects by helping to empower the victims. Of course, this is a small sample with no comparison group, so one can neither generalize from this research nor attribute the changes to the shelter. Other studies that examined the effect of shelters suffer from the same methodological problems and cannot be used to determine whether women who return to their husbands after a shelter stay are at greater or lesser risk for abuse.

A study by the sociologists Richard Berk, Phyllis Newton, and Sarah Fenstermaker Berk (1986) followed 243 wife battery victims in Santa Barbara, California. At the end of 18 months, they were still in contact with 155 of the victims. Using the records from a shelter, the researchers were able to determine which of the 243 victims had stayed in the shelter between the time of the first and second interviews. Fifty-seven women had used a shelter, staying between 1 and 30 days. Based on their interviews, the investigators concluded that shelters appear to have a beneficial effect. However, the benefits depend on the attitudes of the women. When a victim can actually take control of her life, a shelter stay can dramatically reduce the likelihood of new violence. More than 8 of the 10 women who stayed at a shelter experienced no new violence between the time they left the shelter and when they were interviewed (an average of 54 days). For women who cannot take control of their lives, shelters either have no effect or, worse, may actually trigger retaliation from an angry partner or husband. Five percent of the women who left the shelter were beaten more than once after returning home.

Berk and his associates caution that theirs is but a single study with some important methodological limitations. It would be premature, the researchers argue, to base major policy changes on this single study. The study does, however, illuminate the fact that the effect of shelters is not uniform for all victims of wife battery.

Edward Gondolf and Ellen Fisher (1988) studied a sample of 1,482 battered women in shelters and 650 battered women who were using non-residential shelter-based programs in Texas. They concluded that shelters play a pivotal role in facilitating helpseeking. Victims of domestic violence used shelters for much more than just refuge. The most-used services were counseling, transportation, and referral.

Ending a violent relationship is a major life change for women, and most women do not leave a violent relationship after only one shelter stay. Women often do return to their partners after a shelter stay, and women may stay in a shelter a number of times before choosing to leave a violent partner for good.

Men's treatment programs. Since 1980, there has been enormous growth in the number and variety of treatment programs for men who batter. Beginning with EMERGE in Boston in 1977, Brother to Brother in Providence, Rhode Island, and AMEND in Denver, organizations around the country have been created with the goal of counseling violent men.

Treatment programs for men who batter vary in many respects. The majority are court mandated. Others are self-help and depend on self-referrals. A third type of program operates within private social service or substance abuse treatment agencies.

The vast majority of programs are group treatment programs. The underlying philosophy, operational characteristics, and length of programs vary. Many group treatment programs are psychoeducational, with many having an underlying pro-feminist orientation to the problem of woman assault (Edleson & Tolman, 1992). A psychoeducational approach focuses on asking men to accept responsibility for their abuse and ending the violence. The underlying feminist approach includes an examination of how patriarchy and men's attitudes and behavior about control lead to the abuse and battering of women. Feminist intervention programs target men's images about what it means to be male and the belief that they should control their wives or partners. Men also examine the various physical and nonphysical methods they use to control wives and partners. As with feminist theory of the causes of violence against women (see Chapter 6), power and control are the key issues in feminist treatment programs for men.

Many treatment programs emphasize anger management for the men in the groups. Anger management techniques include teaching men to recognize and manage their anger by recognizing cues and then using a technique to control the anger. Anger management responses include taking a "time-out," using a relaxing technique, or using a cognitive technique such as "self talk."

The length of treatment programs tend to vary, but most are short-term, ranging in length from 6 to 32 weeks (Edleson & Tolman, 1992).

One of the problems with group treatment programs for men is that drop-out rates tend to be high: from one third to two thirds (Saunders & Hanusa, 1986).

There have been only a few empirical evaluations of treatment programs for men who batter that have used appropriate control or comparison
groups and long enough follow-up periods to determine the effectiveness
of the various types and structures of treatment programs. Thus, we do not
know whether such programs are actually effective; which type of treatment program is most effective (e.g., anger management, psychoeducational, feminist, or some combination of these models); and what length
of program is most effective. Most advocates believe that programs must
be longer than 26 weeks, but there are no data yet to support such a belief.

At the moment, we know that treatment programs have low recruitment
rates and high drop-out rates. We cannot confidently say, however, that
overall, such treatment programs work at reducing violence and abuse or
that a specific type of program is more effective than others (Hamberger
& Hastings, 1993; Rosenfeld, 1992).

There is an important caution regarding treatment programs for men
who batter. Gondolf and Fisher (1988) found that a batterer seeking
counseling is the most influential predictor of whether his wife or partner
will return to him after leaving a shelter. Given the lack of evidence demonstrating the efficacy of treatment programs for men who batter, these
data suggest that the existence of such programs may actually *increase a
woman's risk* by creating a false sense of hope among those women whose
partners have sought treatment.

Couples counseling. The most controversial treatment for domestic violence
is couples counseling or what some call "family systems" treatment (Neidig,
Friedman, & Collins, 1985). The main assumption of a systems or couples
approach is that relationship violence is a "symptom of dysfunctional
interactions in a couple's relationship." Violent episodes are seen as part of
an interaction sequence in which both batterer and victim contribute to an
escalation of tension that ends in a violent outburst (Harris, Savage, Jones, &
Brooke, 1988, p. 148). Because this approach views violence as a relationship
issue, counseling usually includes the wife or partner in therapy.

Couples counseling and systems therapy have been vigorously criti-
cized, and many advocates for victims state that couples therapy is never
appropriate. Critics charge that couples counseling implies, implicitly or
explicitly, that the woman is, in some way, responsible for the violence
and battering and that such an approach is an example of "victim blaming."
Women, critics argue, may be placed at risk by being required to par-

ticipate in couples therapy because a husband or partner may retaliate for things said during the therapy session. Finally, systems theory is thought to ignore gender issues and the significant issues of power, control, and patriarchy that are at the core of domestic violence (Adams, 1988; Bograd, 1984).

Other Forms of Intimate Violence

As I noted in Chapter 5, violent intimate relations other than parent to child and husband to wife have long been hidden from public attention. Thus, with only rare exceptions, there are no treatment programs for offenders or victims of sibling violence and violence toward parents (with the exception of violence toward elders). If these forms of violence are recognized and treated at all, they typically are dealt with through traditional individual and family counseling.

Mandatory elder abuse reporting laws exist in 42 states. The laws vary from state to state, and the results have been mixed. Funding and staffing for mandatory adult protective services laws is often quite limited. Adult protective services workers have found that elderly victims of violence have been extremely reluctant to leave violent and abusive homes. The fear of being institutionalized seems to outweigh the pain and suffering some elderly victims experience. Thus, adult protective services workers often invest countless hours investigating reports of elder abuse, only to find the victim reluctant to accept any form of treatment.

There are a limited number of self-help groups for victims of elder abuse. Most parents still seem to be suffering in silence and shame. Violent siblings, unless they maim or kill a brother or sister, are not even recognized as violent, let alone attended to with treatment or intervention.

Prevention

Treatment is necessary to protect the lives and welfare of the victims or potential victims of intimate violence. But even the implementation of effective and efficient treatment programs will not break the cycle of cultural norms and values that contribute to the violent nature of the family and intimate relationships. Nor do treatment programs alone alter the characteristics of society and the family that increase the risk that certain relationships will be violent and abusive.

The central goal of programs and policies aimed at intimate violence is to prevent violence. The findings presented in this book clearly point to the fact that some fundamental changes in values and beliefs will have to occur before we see a real decrease in the level of violence in the intimate relationships. Looking toward the future, there are a number of policy steps that could help prevent intimate violence.

---

1. *Eliminate the norms that legitimize and glorify violence in the society and the family.* The elimination of spanking as a child-rearing technique; gun control, to get deadly weapons out of the home; elimination of corporal punishment in school; elimination of the death penalty; and an elimination of media violence that glorifies and legitimizes violence are all necessary steps. In short, we need to cancel the hitting license in society.

---

2. *Reduce violence-provoking stress created by society.* Reducing poverty, inequality, and unemployment and providing for adequate housing, feeding, medical and dental care, and educational opportunities are steps that could reduce stress in families.

---

3. *Integrate families into a network of kin and community.* Reducing social isolation would be a significant step that would help reduce stress and increase the abilities of families to manage stress.

---

4. *Change the sexist character of society.* Sexual inequality makes violence possible in homes. The elimination of men's work and women's work would be a major step toward equality in and out of the home.

---

5. *Break the cycle of violence in the family.* This step repeats the message of Step 1—violence cannot be prevented as long as we are taught that it is appropriate to hit the people we love. Physical punishment of children is perhaps the most effective means of teaching violence, and eliminating it would be an important step in violence prevention.

Such steps require long-term changes in the fabric of society. These proposals call for such fundamental change in families and family life that many people resist them and argue that they could not work or would ruin the family. The alternative, of course, is that not making such changes continues the harmful and deadly tradition of intimate violence.

Note

1. *Substantiated* means that the allegation of maltreatment or the risk of maltreatment was supported or "founded" on the basis of state law. *Indicated* means that maltreatment could not be substantiated, but there is reason to believe that the child was maltreated or at risk of maltreatment (U.S. Department of Health and Human Services, National Center on Child Abuse and Neglect, 1996).

DISCUSSION QUESTIONS

1. How do police expectations about battered women being prone to drop charges against their abusive husbands create a self-fulfilling prophecy and deny women their proper legal rights of protection?

2. What legal remedies could be enacted to deal with the problems of hidden family violence—elder abuse, sibling violence, parent abuse, and abuse of adolescents?

3. Give an example of how compassion and control could be used to intervene in cases of child abuse, wife abuse, and elder abuse.

SUGGESTED ASSIGNMENTS

1. Create a resource guide that lists the community services (names, addresses, and telephone numbers) of agencies and organizations that deal with various aspects of family violence.

2. Find out what the local laws are about domestic violence and see how they are implemented by observing in a courtroom.

REFERENCES

Aber, J. L., Allen, J. P., Carlson V., & Cicchetti, D. (1990). The effects of maltreatment on development during early childhood: Recent studies and their theoretical, clinical, and ⌐ icy implications. In D. Cicchetti & V. Carlson (Eds.), *Child maltreatment: Theory and research on causes and consequences* (pp. 579-619). New York: Cambridge University Press.

Adams, D. (1988). Treatment models of men who batter: A pro-feminist analysis. In K. Yllö & M. Bograd (Eds.), *Feminist perspectives on wife abuse* (pp. 176-199). Newbury Park, CA: Sage.

Adelson, L. (1972). The battering child. *Journal of the American Medical Association, 222,* 159-161.

Agnew, R., & Huguley, S. (1989). Adolescent violence towards parents. *Journal of Marriage and the Family, 51,* 699-711.

American Association for Protecting Children. (1988). *Highlights of official child neglect and abuse reporting, 1986.* Denver, CO: American Humane Association.

American Association for Protecting Children. (1989). *Highlights of official child neglect and abuse reporting, 1987.* Denver, CO: American Humane Association.

American Humane Association. (1976). *National analysis of official child neglect and abuse reporting, 1974.* Denver, CO: Author.

American Humane Association. (1984). *Trends in child abuse and neglect: A national perspective.* Denver, CO: Author.

Ammerman, R. T. (1991). The role of the child in physical abuse: A reappraisal. *Violence and Victims, 6,* 87-100.

169

Arias, I., Samois, M., & O'Leary, K. D. (1987). Prevalence and correlates of physical aggression during courtship. *Journal of Interpersonal Violence, 2*, 82-90.

Aries, P. (1962). *Centuries of childhood.* New York: Knopf.

Bachman, R. (1994). *Violence against women: A National Crime Victimization Survey report.* Washington: U.S. Department of Justice, Bureau of Justice Statistics.

Bachman, R., & Saltzman, L. (1995). *Violence against women: Estimates from the redesigned survey.* Washington, DC: U.S. Department of Justice, Bureau of Justice Statistics.

Ball, M. (1977). Issues of violence in family casework. *Social Casework, 58*, 3-12.

Bard, M. (1971). The study and modification of intra-family violence. In J. L. Singer (Ed.), *The control of aggression and violence* (pp. 149-164). New York: Academic Press.

Barnett, O. W., & LaViolette, A. D. (1993). *It could happen to anyone: Why battered women stay.* Newbury Park, CA: Sage.

Barthel, J. (1991). *For children's sake: The promise of family preservation.* New York: Edna McConnell Clark Foundation.

The battered-child syndrome. (1962). *Journal of the American Medical Association, 181*, 42.

Belsky, J. (1980). Child maltreatment: An ecological integration. *American Psychologist, 35*, 320-335.

Belsky, J. (1993). Etiology of child maltreatment: A developmental-ecological analysis. *Psychological Bulletin, 114*, 413-434.

Bender, L. (1959). Children and adolescents who have killed. *American Journal of Psychiatry, 116*, 510-513.

Berk, R., Berk, S. F., Loseke, D. R., & Rauma, D. (1983). Mutual combat and other family violence myths. In D. Finkelhor, R. J. Gelles, G. T. Hotaling, & M. A. Straus (Eds.), *The dark side of families: Current family violence research* (pp. 197-212). Beverly Hills, CA: Sage.

Berk, R., Newton, P., & Berk, S. F. (1986). What a difference a day makes: An empirical study of the impact of shelters for battered women. *Journal of Marriage and the Family, 48*, 481-490.

Berk, R. A., Campbell, A., Klap, R., & Western, B. (1992). The deterrent effect of arrest incidents of domestic violence: A Bayesian analysis of four field experiments. *American Sociological Review, 57*, 698-708.

Berk, S., & Loseke, D. (1980). "Handling" family violence: The situated determinants of police arrest in domestic disturbances. *Law and Society Review, 15*, 317-346.

Besharov, D. J. (1993). Overreporting and underreporting are twin problems. In R. J. Gelles & D. Loseke (Eds.), *Current controversies on family violence* (pp. 257-272). Newbury Park, CA: Sage.

Blau, P. M. (1964). *Exchange and power in social life.* New York: Wiley.

Block, M., & Sinnott, J. (1979). *Battered elder syndrome: An exploratory study.* Unpublished manuscript, University of Maryland.

Blumberg, M. (1964). When parents hit out. *Twentieth Century, 173*, 39-44.

Bograd, M. (1984). Family systems approaches to wife battering: A feminist critique. *American Journal of Orthopsychiatry, 54*, 558-568.

Bowker, L. H. (1983). *Beating wife-beating.* Lexington, MA: Lexington Books.

Bowker, L. H. (1993). A battered woman's problems are social, not psychological. In R. J. Gelles & D. Loseke (Eds.), *Current controversies on family violence* (pp. 154-165). Newbury Park, CA: Sage.

Brand, P. A., & Kidd, A. H. (1986). Frequency of physical aggression in heterosexual and female homosexual dyads. *Psychological Reports, 59*, 1307-1313.

Brekke, J., & Saunders, D. (1982). *Research on woman abuse: A review of findings, needs, and issues.* Unpublished manuscript.

Bronfenbrenner, U. (1958). Socialization and social class throughout time and space. In E. Maccoby et al. (Eds.), *Readings in social psychology* (pp. 400-425). Rockville, MD: Westat.

Brott, A. (1994, August 6). Abused statistics can also hurt. *Providence Journal Bulletin,* p. A8.

Browne, A. (1987). *When battered women kill.* New York: Free Press.

Browne, A., & Finkelhor, D. (1986). Initial and long-term effects: A review of research. In D. Finkelhor & Associates (Eds.), *A sourcebook on child sexual abuse* (pp. 143-179). Beverly Hills, CA: Sage.

Burgdorf, K. (1980). *Recognition and reporting of child maltreatment.* Rockville, MD: Westat.

Burgess, R. L. (1979, November). *Family violence: Some implications from evolutionary biology.* Paper presented at the annual meetings of the American Society of Criminology, Philadelphia.

Burgess, R. L., & Garbarino, J. (1983). Doing what comes naturally? An evolutionary perspective on child abuse. In D. Finkelhor, R. J. Gelles, G. T. Hotaling, & M. A. Straus (Eds.), *The dark side of families: Current family violence research* (pp. 88-101). Beverly Hills, CA: Sage.

Caffey, J. (1946). Multiple fractures in the long bones of infants suffering from chronic subdural hematoma. *American Journal of Roentgenology, Radium Therapy, and Nuclear Medicine, 58*, 163-173.

Caffey, J. (1957). Some traumatic lesions in growing bones other than fractures and dislocations. *British Journal of Radiology, 23*, 225-238.

Campbell, J. C. (1992). "If I can't have you, no one can": Issues of power and control in domestic homicide. In J. Radford & D. Russell (Eds.), *Femicide: The politics of woman killing* (pp. 99-113). New York: Twayne.

Cochran, D., Brown, M. E., Adams, S. L., & Doherty, D. (1994). *Young adolescent batterers: A profile of restraining order defendants in Massachusetts.* Boston: Massachusetts Trial Court, Office of the Commissioner of Probation.

Coleman, D., & Straus, M. (1983). Alcohol abuse and family violence. In E. Gottheil, K. Druley, T. Skoloda, & H. Waxman (Eds.), *Alcohol, drug abuse and aggression* (pp. 104-124). Springfield, IL: Charles C Thomas.

Connelley, C. D., & Straus, M. A. (1992). Mother's age and risk for child abuse. *Child Abuse & Neglect: The International Journal, 16*, 703-712.

Conte, J. (1984, July). *Research on the prevention of sexual abuse of children.* Paper presented at the Second National Conference for Family Violence Researchers, Durham, NH.

Cornell, C. P., & Gelles, R. J. (1982). Adolescent to parent violence. *Urban Social Change Review, 15*, 8-14.

Counts, D., Brown, J., & Campbell, J. C. (1992). *Sanctions and sanctuary: Cultural perspectives on the beating of wives*. Boulder, CO: Westview.

Curtis, L. (1974). *Criminal violence: National patterns and behavior*. Lexington, MA: Lexington Books.

D'Agostino, S. (1983, August 17). Finally, judgement. *Worcester Magazine*, pp. 11-13.

Daly, M., & Wilson, M. (1980). Discriminative parental solicitude: A biosocial perspective. *Journal of Marriage and the Family, 42*, 277-288.

Daly, M., & Wilson, M. (1981). Child maltreatment from a sociobiological perspective. *New Directions for Child Development, 11*, 93-112.

Daly, M., & Wilson, M. (1985). Child abuse and other risks of not living with both parents. *Ethology and Sociobiology, 6*, 197-210.

Daly, M., & Wilson, M. (1987). Children as homicide victims. In R. J. Gelles & J. B. Lancaster (Eds.), *Child abuse and neglect: Biosocial dimensions* (pp. 201-214). Hawthorne, NY: Aldine de Gruyter.

Daly, M., & Wilson, M. (1988a). Evolutionary social psychology and family homicide. *Science, 242*, 524.

Daly, M., & Wilson, M. (1988b). *Homicide*. New York: Aldine de Gruyter.

Daro, D. (1988). *Confronting child abuse: Research for effective programming*. New York: Free Press.

Daro, D. (1995). *Public opinion and behaviors regarding child abuse prevention: The results of NCPCA's 1995 public opinion poll*. Chicago: National Committee to Prevent Child Abuse.

Daro, D., & Gelles, R. (1992). Public attitudes and behaviors with respect to child abuse prevention. *Journal of Interpersonal Violence, 7*, 517-531.

Dawson, J. M., & Langan, P. A. (1994). *Murder in families*. Washington, DC: Bureau of Justice Statistics.

DeMause, L. (Ed.). (1974). *The history of childhood*. New York: Psychohistory Press.

Dobash, R. E., & Dobash, R. (1979). *Violence against wives*. New York: Free Press.

Dodge, K. A., Bates, J. E., & Pettit, G. S. (1990). Mechanisms in the cycle of violence. *Science, 250*, 1678-1683.

Domestic Violence Research Group. (1993, June). *A study of violence precipitated by husbands (boyfriends) in Japan: Preliminary findings*. Paper presented at the NGO parallel activities at the United Nations World Conference on Human Rights, Vienna, Austria.

Dunford, F. W., Huizinga, D., & Elliott, D. (1990). The role of arrest in domestic assault: The Omaha Police Experiment. *Criminology, 28*, 183-206.

Dutton, D. G., & Golant, S. K. (1995). *The batterer: A psychological profile*. New York: Basic Books.

Dutton, D. G., & Starzomski, A. J. (1993). Borderline personality in perpetrators of psychological and physical violence. *Violence and Victims, 8*, 327-337.

Edleson J. L., & Tolman, R. M. (1992). *Intervention for men who batter: An ecological approach*. Newbury Park, CA: Sage.

Egeland, B., Breitenbucher, M., & Rosenberg, D. (1980). A prospective study of the significance of life stress in the etiology of child abuse. *Journal of Clinical and Consulting Psychology, 48*, 195-205.

Egeland, B., Jacobvitz, D., & Papatola, K. (1987). Intergenerational continuity of abuse. In R. J. Gelles & J. B. Lancaster (Eds.), *Child abuse and neglect: Biosocial dimensions* (pp. 255-276). Hawthorne, New York: Aldine de Gruyter.

Egeland, B., Jacobvitz, D., & Sroufe, L. A. (1988). Breaking the cycle of abuse. *Child Development, 59,* 1080-1088.

Egeland, B., & Sroufe, L. A. (1981). Attachment and early child maltreatment. *Child Development, 52, 44-52.*

Elliott, D. S. (1989). Criminal justice procedures in family violence crimes. In L. Ohlin & M. Tonry (Eds.), *Family violence* (pp. 427-480). Chicago: University of Chicago Press.

Elmer, E. (1967). *Children in jeopardy: A study of abused minors and their families.* Pittsburgh, PA: University of Pittsburgh Press.

English, D. (1993, March). *Children who sexually abuse other children: Research findings from three studies.* Paper presented at the Sixth Annual Research Conference. A System of Care for Children's Mental Health: Expanding the Research Base, Tampa, FL.

Erlanger, H. (1974). Social class and corporal punishment in childrearing: A reassessment. *American Sociological Review, 39,* 68-85.

Etzioni, A. (1971). Violence. In R. K. Merton & R. Nisbet (Eds.), *Contemporary social problems* (pp. 709-741). New York: Harcourt Brace Jovanovich.

Evans, E. D., & Warren-Sohlberg, L. A. (1988). A pattern of adolescent abusive behavior towards parents. *Journal of Adolescent Research, 3,* 201-216.

Fagan, J. A. (1990). Intoxication and aggression. In M. Tonry & J. Q. Wilson (Eds.), *Drugs and crime: Vol. 13. Crime and justice: An annual review* (pp. 241-320). Chicago: University of Chicago Press.

Fagan, J. A., & Browne, A. (1994). Violence between spouses and intimates: Physical aggression between women and men in intimate relationships. In A. J. Reiss, Jr. & J. A. Roth (Eds.), *Understanding and preventing violence* (Vol. 3, pp. 115-292). Washington, DC: National Academy Press.

Fagan, J. A., Stewart, D. K., & Stewart, K. W. (1983). Situational correlates of domestic and extra-domestic violence. In D. Finkelhor, R. J. Gelles, G. T. Hotaling, & M. A. Straus (Eds.), *The dark side of families: Current family violence research* (pp. 49-67). Beverly Hills, CA: Sage.

Family Violence Prevention Fund. (1995). Poll finds rising concern about abuse. *Speaking Up, 1,* 1ff.

Farrell, W. (1994, June 29). Spouse abuse: A two way street. *USA Today,* p. 15A.

Feld, S. L., & Straus, M. A. (1989). Escalation and desistance of violence in marriage. *Criminology, 27,* 141-161.

Fergusson, D. M., Fleming, J., & O'Neil, D. (1972). *Child abuse in New Zealand.* Wellington, New Zealand: Research Division, Department of Social Work.

Ferreira, A. (1963). Family myth and homeostasis. *Archives of General Psychiatry, 9,* 451-463.

Field, M., & Field, H. (1973). Marital violence and the criminal process: Neither justice nor peace. *Social Service Review, 47,* 221-240.

Figgie Report: *The Figgie Report on Fear of Crime: American Afraid,* Part I, The General Public. (1980). Willoughby, OH: A-T-O.

Finkelhor, D. (1979). *Sexually victimized children.* New York: Free Press.

Finkelhor, D. (1983). Common features of family abuse. In D. Finkelhor, R. J. Gelles, G. T. Hotaling, & M. A. Straus (Eds.), *The dark side of families: Current family violence research* (pp. 17-28). Beverly Hills, CA: Sage.

Finkelhor, D. (1984). *Child sexual abuse: New theory and research*. New York: Free Press.

Finkelhor, D. (1987). The sexual abuse of children: Current research reviewed. *Psychiatric Annals, 17*, 233-241.

Finkelhor, D. (1993). The main problem is still underreporting, not overreporting. In R. J. Gelles & D. Loseke (Eds.), *Current controversies on family violence* (pp. 273-287). Newbury Park, CA: Sage.

Finkelhor, D., & Dziuba-Leatherman, J. (1994a). Children as victims of violence. A national study. *Pediatrics, 94*, 413-420.

Finkelhor, D., & Dziuba-Leatherman, J. (1994b). Victimization of children. *American Psychologist, 49*, 173-183.

Finkelhor, D., Hotaling, G., Lewis, I. A., & Smith, C. (1990). Sexual abuse in a national survey of adult men and women: Prevalence, characteristics, and risk factors. *Child Abuse & Neglect: The International Journal, 14*, 19-28.

Finkelhor, D., & Korbin, J. (1988). Child abuse as an international issue. *Child Abuse & Neglect: The International Journal, 12*, 3-23.

Finkelhor, D., & Yllö, K. (1985). *License to rape: Sexual abuse of wives*. New York: Holt, Rinehart & Winston.

Fontana, V. (1973). *Somewhere a child is crying: Maltreatment—causes and prevention*. New York: Macmillan.

Ford, D. (1991). Preventing and provoking wife battery through criminal sanctions: A look at the risks. In D. D. Knudson & J. L. Miller (Eds.), *Abused and battered: Social and legal responses to family violence* (pp. 191-209). New York: Aldine de Gruyter.

Forsythe, P. (1992). Homebuilders and family preservation. *Children and Youth Services Review, 14*, 37-47.

Friederich, W. N. (1988). Behavior problems in sexually abused children. In G. E. Wyatt & G. J. Powell (Eds), *The lasting effects of child sexual abuse* (pp. 171-191). Newbury Park, CA: Sage.

Friederich, W. N., & Boriskin, J. A. (1976). The role of the child in abuse: A review of literature. *American Journal of Orthopsychiatry, 46*, 580-590.

Gallup Organization. (1995). *Disciplining children in America*. Princeton, NJ: Author.

Garbarino, J. (1977). The human ecology of child maltreatment. *Journal of Marriage and the Family, 39*, 721-735.

Gayford, J. J. (1975). Wife battering: A preliminary survey of 100 cases. *British Medical Journal, 1*, 194-197.

Gelles, R. J. (1974). *The violent home*. Beverly Hills, CA: Sage.

Gelles, R. J. (1976). Abused wives: Why do they stay? *Journal of Marriage and the Family, 38*, 659-668.

Gelles, R. J. (1989). Child abuse and violence in single parent families: Parent absence and economic deprivation. *American Journal of Orthopsychiatry, 59*, 492-501.

Gelles, R. J. (1992). Poverty and violence toward children. *American Behavioral Scientist, 35*, 258-264.

Gelles, R. J. (1993). Alcohol and other drugs are associated with violence—They are not its cause. In R. J. Gelles & D. Loseke (Eds.), *Current controversies on family violence* (pp. 182-196). Newbury Park, CA: Sage.

Gelles, R. J. (1995). *Family violence by income.* Unpublished data. Kingston, RI. (Mimeographed)

Gelles, R. J. (1996). *The book of David: How preserving families can cost children's lives.* New York: Basic Books.

Gelles, R. J., & Cornell, C. (Eds.). (1983). *International perspectives on family violence.* Lexington, MA: Lexington Books.

Gelles, R. J., & Edfeldt, A. (1986). Violence towards children in the United States and Sweden. *Child Abuse & Neglect: The International Journal, 10,* 501-510.

Gelles, R. J., & Hargreaves, E. (1981). Maternal employment and violence towards children. *Journal of Family Issues, 2,* 509-530.

Gelles, R. J., & Harrop, J. W. (1991). The risk of abusive violence among children with non-biological parents. *Family Relations, 40,* 78-83.

Gelles, R. J., & Straus, M. A. (1979). Determinants of violence in the family: Toward a theoretical integration. In W. R. Burr, R. Hill, F. I. Nye, & I. L. Reiss (Eds.), *Contemporary theories about the family* (Vol. 1, pp. 549-581). New York: Free Press.

Gelles, R. J., & Straus, M. A. (1987). Is violence towards children increasing? A comparison of 1975 and 1985 national survey rates. *Journal of Interpersonal Violence, 2,* 212-222.

Gelles, R. J., & Straus, M. A. (1988). *Intimate violence.* New York: Simon & Schuster.

Gelles, R. J., Wolfner, G. D., & Lackner, R. (1994). Men who batter: The risk markers. *Violence Update, 4,* 1ff.

Gil, D. (1970). *Violence against children: Physical child abuse in the United States.* Cambridge, MA: Harvard University Press.

Gilbert, N. (1993). Examining the facts: Advocacy research overstates the incidence of date and acquaintance rape. In R. J. Gelles & D. Loseke (Eds.), *Current controversies on family violence* (pp. 120-132). Newbury Park, CA: Sage.

Giles-Sims, J. (1983). *Wife-beating: A systems theory approach.* New York: Guilford.

Giles-Sims, J., & Finkelhor, D. (1984). Child abuse in stepfamilies. *Family Relations, 33,* 407-413.

Gillen, J. (1946). *The Wisconsin prisoner: Studies in crimogenesis.* Madison: University of Wisconsin Press.

Giovannoni, J. M., & Becerra, R. M. (1979). *Defining child abuse.* New York: Free Press.

Gondolf, E. W., & Fisher, E. R. (1988). *Battered women as survivors: An alternative treating learned helplessness.* Lexington, MA: Lexington Books.

Goode, W. (1971). Force and violence in the family. *Journal of Marriage and the Family, 33,* 624-636.

Goodwin, M. P., & Roscoe, B. (1990). Sibling violence and agonistic interactions among middle adolescents. *Adolescence, 25,* 451-467.

Gordon, M. (1989). The family environment and sexual abuse: A comparison of natal and stepfather abuse. *Child Abuse & Neglect: The International Journal, 13,* 121-129.

Gordon, M., & Creighton, S. J. (1988). Natal and non-natal fathers sexual abusers in the United Kingdom: A comparative analysis. *Journal of Marriage and the Family, 50,* 99-105.

Greven, P. (1990). *Spare the child: The religious roots of punishment and the psychological impact of physical abuse*. New York: Knopf.

Guttmacher, M. (1960). *The mind of the murderer*. New York: Farrar, Straus, and Cudahy.

Hagedorn, J. M. (1995). *Forsaking our children: Bureaucracy and reform in the child welfare system*. Chicago: Lake View.

Hamberger, L. K., & Hastings, J. E. (1986). Personality correlates of men who abuse their partners: A cross-validation study. *Journal of Family Violence, 1*, 232-346.

Hamberger, L. K., & Hastings, J. E. (1991). Personality correlates of men who batter and non-violent men. Some continuities and discontinuities. *Journal of Family Violence, 6*, 131-147.

Hamberger, L. K., & Hastings, J. E. (1993). Court-mandated treatment of men who batter their partners: Issues, controversies, and outcomes. In Z. Hilton (Ed.), *Legal responses to wife assault* (pp. 188-229). Newbury Park, CA: Sage.

Hampton, R. L., & Gelles, R. J. (1994). Violence toward Black women in a nationally representative sample of Black families. *Journal of Comparative Family Studies, 25*, 105-119.

Hampton, R. L., Gelles, R. J., & Harrop, J. W. (1989). Is violence in Black families increasing? A comparison of 1975 and 1985 national survey rates. *Journal of Marriage and the Family, 51*, 969-980.

Hampton, R. L., & Newberger, E. H. (1985). Child abuse incidence and reporting by hospitals: The significance of severity, class, and race. *American Journal of Public Health, 75*, 56-60.

Harbin, H., & Madden, D. (1979). Battered parents: A new syndrome. *American Journal of Psychiatry, 136*, 1288-1291.

Harris, R., Savage, S., Jones, T., & Brooke, W. (1988). A comparison of treatments for abusive men and their partners within a family-service agency. *Canadian Journal of Community Mental Health, 7*, 147-155.

Hart, S. D., Dutton, D. G., & Newlove, T. (1993). The prevalence of personality disorder among wife assaulters. *Journal of Personality Disorders, 7*, 328-340.

Hastings, J. E., & Hamberger, L. K. (1988). Personality characteristics of spouse abusers: A controlled study. *Violence and Victims, 3*, 31-48.

Haugaard, J. (1994). Sexual abuse in families. In L. L'Abate (Ed.), *Handbook of developmental family psychology and psychopathology* (pp. 309-329). New York: Wiley.

Hegar, R. L., Zuravin, S. J., & Orme, J. G. (1994). Factors predicting severity of physical child abuse injury: A review of the literature. *Journal of Interpersonal Violence, 9*, 170-183.

Heide, K. M. (1989). Parricide: Incidence and issues. *The Justice Professional, 4*, 19-41.

Heide, K. M. (1995). *Why kids kill parents: Child abuse and adolescent homicide*. Thousand Oaks, CA: Sage.

Heise, L. L. (1994). *Violence against women: The hidden health burden*. World Bank Discussion Papers No. 255. Washington, DC: World Bank.

Heneghan, A. M., Horwitz, S. M., & Leventhal, J. M. (1996). Evaluating intensive family preservation programs: A methodological review. *Pediatrics, 97*, 535-542.

Henton, J., Cate, R., Koval, J., Lloyd, S., & Christopher, S. (1983). Romance and violence in dating relationships. *Journal of Family Issues, 4*, 467-482.

Herrenkohl, E. C., Herrenkohl, R. C., & Toedler, L. J. (1983). Perspectives on the intergenerational transmission of abuse. In D. Finkelhor, R. J. Gelles, G. T. Hotaling, & M. A. Straus (Eds.), *The dark side of families: Current family violence research* (pp. 305-316). Beverly Hills, CA: Sage.

Hilberman, E. (1980). Overview: "The wife-beater's wife" reconsidered. *American Journal of Psychiatry, 137,* 1336-1346.

Hilberman, E., & Munson, K. (1977). Sixty battered women. *Victimology, 2,* 460-470.

Hirschell, J. D., Hutchinson, I. W., III, & Dean, C.W. (1990). The failure of arrest to deter spouse abuse. *Journal of Research in Crime and Delinquency, 29,* 7-33.

Hornung, C., McCullough, B., & Sugimoto, T. (1981). Status relationships in marriage: Risk factors in spouse abuse. *Journal of Marriage and the Family, 43,* 679-692.

Hotaling, G., & Sugarman, D. (1986). An analysis of risk markers in husband to wife violence. *Violence and Victims, 1,* 101-124.

Hotaling, G., & Sugarman, D. (1990). A risk marker analysis of assaulted wives. *Journal of Family Violence, 5,* 1-13.

Hrdy, S. B. (1979). Infanticide among animals: A review of classification, and examination of implications for reproductive strategies for females. *Ethology and Sociobiology, 1,* 13-40.

Hunter, R., & Kilstrom, N. (1979). Breaking the cycle of abusive families. *American Journal of Psychiatry, 136,* 1320-1322.

Hunter, R., Kilstrom, N., Kraybill, E. N., & Loda, F. (1978). Antecedents of child abuse and neglect in premature infants: A prospective study in a newborn intensive care unit. *Pediatrics, 61,* 629-635.

Hwalek, M., Senstock, M. C., & Lawrence, R. (1984, November). *Assessing the probability of abuse of the elderly.* Paper presented at the annual meetings of the Gerontological Society of America, San Antonio, TX.

Hyman, A. (1995). *Reporting of domestic violence by health care providers: Overview of state statutes.* San Francisco: Family Violence Prevention Fund.

Isaac, N., Cochran, D., Brown, M. E., & Adams, S. L. (1994). Men who batter: Profile from a restraining order data base. *Archives of Family Medicine, 3,* 50-54.

Jacobson, N. (1993). *Domestic violence: What are the marriages like?* Anaheim, CA: American Association for Marriage and Family Therapy.

Johnson, C. (1974). *Child abuse in the southeast: An analysis of 1172 reported cases.* Athens, GA: Welfare Research.

Johnson, R. (1972). *Aggression in man and animals.* Philadelphia: W.B. Saunders.

Jones, A. (1980). *Women who kill.* New York: Holt, Rinehart & Winston.

Kaufman, J., & Zigler, E. (1987). Do abused children become abusive parents? *American Journal of Orthopsychiatry, 57,* 186-192.

Kaufman, J., & Zigler, E. (1993). The intergenerational transmission of abuse is overstated. In R. J. Gelles & D. Loseke (Eds.), *Current controversies on family violence* (pp. 209-221). Newbury Park, CA: Sage.

Kaufman Kantor, G., & Straus, M. A. (1987). The drunken bum theory of wife beating. *Social Problems, 34,* 213-230.

Kempe, C. H., Silverman, F. N., Steele, B. F., Droegemueller, W., & Silver, H. K. (1962). The battered child syndrome. *Journal of the American Medical Association, 181,* 107-112.

Kendall-Tackett, K. A., Williams, L., & Finkelhor, D. (1993). The impact of sexual abuse on children: A review and synthesis of recent empirical literature. *Psychological Bulletin, 113*, 164-180.

Kim, K., & Cho, Y. (1992). Epidemiological survey of spousal abuse in Korea. In E. Viano (Ed.), *Intimate violence: Interdisciplinary perspectives* (pp. 277-282). Washington, DC: Hemisphere.

Kinard, M., & Klerman, L. V. (1980). Teenage parenting and child abuse: Are they related? *American Journal of Orthopsychiatry, 50*, 481-488.

Kivela, S.-L., Kongas-Saviaro, P., Kesti, E., Pahkala, K., & Ijas, M. L. (1992). Abuse in old age: Epidemiological data from Finland. *Journal of Elder Abuse & Neglect, 6*, 1-18.

Koch, L., & Koch, J. (1980, January 27). Parent abuse—A new plague. *Washington Post*, pp. A14-A15.

Kohn, M. (1977). *Class and conformity: A study of values.* Chicago: University of Chicago Press.

Korbin, J. (Ed.). (1981). *Child abuse and neglect: Cross-cultural perspectives.* Berkeley: University of California Press.

Koss, M. P., & Cook, S. L. (1993). Facing the facts: Date and acquaintance rape are significant problems for women. In R. J. Gelles & D. Loseke (Eds.), *Current controversies on family violence* (pp. 104-119). Newbury Park, CA: Sage.

Koss, M. P., Gidycz, C. A., & Wisniewski, N. (1987). The scope of rape: Incidence and prevalence of sexual aggression in a national sample of higher education students. *Journal of Consulting and Clinical Psychology, 55*, 162-170.

Lane, K. E., & Gwartney-Gibbs, P. A. (1985). Violence in the context of dating and sex. *Journal of Family Issues, 6*, 45-59.

Lanning, K. V. (1992). *Investigator's guide to allegations of ritual abuse.* Quantico, VA: National Center for the Analysis of Violent Crime.

Larrain, S. (1993). *Estudio de frecuencia de la violencia intrafamiliar y la condicion de la mujer en Chile* [Study of the frequency of intrafamiliar violence and the condition of women in Chile]. Santiago, Chile: Pan-American Health Organization.

Laslett, B. (1973). Family membership, past and present. *Social Problems, 25*, 476-490.

Laslett, B. (1978). The family as a public and private institution: A historical perspective. *Journal of Marriage and the Family, 35*, 480-492.

Lau E. E., & Kosberg, J. I. (1979). Abuse of the elderly by informal care providers. *Aging, 299*, 10-15.

Legal Research and Services for the Elderly. (1979). *Elder abuse in Massachusetts: A survey of professionals and paraprofessionals.* Unpublished report.

Leibrich, J., Paulin, J., & Ransom, R. (1995). *Hitting home: Men speak about abuse toward women partners.* Wellington, New Zealand: Department of Justice in Association with AGB McNair.

Leo, J. (1994, July 11). Is it a war against women? *U.S. News & World Report*, p. 22.

Leonard, K. E., & Jacob, T. (1988). Alcohol, alcoholism, and family violence. In V. B. Van Hasselt, R. L. Morrison, A. S. Bellack, & M. Hersen (Eds.), *Handbook of family violence* (pp. 383-406). New York: Plenum.

Letellier, P. (1994). Gay and lesbian male domestic violence victimization: Challenges to feminist theory and responses to violence. *Violence and Victims, 9*, 95-106.

Leventhal, J., Horwitz, S., Rude, C., & Steir, D. (1993). Maltreatment of children born to teenage mothers: A comparison between the 1960s and 1980s. *Journal of Pediatrics, 122,* 314-319.

Levine, M., Compaan, C., & Freeman, J. (1994, August). *The prevention of child fatalities associated with child maltreatment.* Unpublished manuscript, State University of New York at Buffalo.

Levine, M., Compaan, C., & Freeman, J. (1995). Maltreatment-related fatalities: Issues of policy and prevention. *Law and Policy, 16,* 449-471.

Levinson, D. (1981). Physical punishment of children and wifebeating in cross-cultural perspective. *Child Abuse & Neglect: The International Journal, 5,* 193-196.

Light, R. J. (1974). Abused and neglected children in America: A study of alternative policies. *Harvard Educational Review, 43,* 556-598.

Lindsey, D. (1994). *The welfare of children.* New York: Oxford University Press.

Lloyd, S. A., & Emery, B. (1994). Physically aggressive conflict in romantic relationships. In D. Cahn (Ed.), *Conflict in personal relationships* (pp. 27-46). Hillsdale, NJ: Lawrence Erlbaum.

Lockhart, L. L., White, B. W., Causby, V., & Isaac, A. (1994). Letting out the secret: Violence in lesbian relationships. *Journal of Interpersonal Violence, 9,* 469-492.

London, J. (1978). Images of violence against women. *Victimology, 2,* 510-524.

Lourie, I. (1977). The phenomenon of the abused adolescent: A clinical study. *Victimology, 2,* 268-276.

Lyman, S., & Scott, M. (1970). *A sociology of the absurd.* New York: Appleton-Century-Crofts.

MacAndrew, C., & Edgerton, R. B. (1969). *Drunken comportment: A social explanation.* Chicago: Aldine.

Makepeace, J. (1981). Courtship violence among college students. *Family Relations, 30,* 97-102.

Mangold, W. D., Jr., & Koski, P. R. (1990). Gender comparisons in the relationship between parental and sibling violence and non family violence. *Journal of Family Violence, 5,* 225-235.

Margolin, G., Sibner, L. G., & Gleberman, L. (1988). Wife battering. In V. B. Van Hasselt, R. L. Morrison, A. S. Bellack, & M. Hersen (Eds.), *Handbook of family violence* (pp. 89-118). New York: Plenum.

Margolin, L. (1991). Abuse and neglect in nonparental child care: A risk assessment. *Journal of Marriage and the Family, 53,* 694-704.

Margolin, L. (1992). Beyond maternal blame: Physical child abuse as a phenomenon of gender. *Journal of Family Issues, 13,* 410-423.

Martin, M. J., & Walters, J. (1982). Familial correlates of selected types of child abuse and neglect. *Journal of Marriage and the Family, 44,* 267-276.

McClain, P., Sacks, J., & Frohlke, R. (1993). Estimates of fatal child abuse and neglect, United States, 1979-1988. *Pediatrics, 91,* 338-343.

McCurdy, K., & Daro, D. (1993). *Current trends in child abuse reporting and fatalities: The results of the 1992 annual fifty state survey.* Chicago: National Center on Child Abuse Prevention Research, National Committee for Prevention of Child Abuse.

Merton, R. K. (1945). Sociological theory. *American Journal of Sociology, 50,* 462-473.

Miller, A. (1983). *For your own good: Hidden cruelty in child-rearing and the roots of violence.* New York: Farrar, Straus, and Giroux.

Mills, C. W. (1940). Situated actions and vocabularies of motive. *American Sociological Review, 5,* 904-913.

Mones, P. (1991). *When a child kills: Abused children who kill their parents.* New York: Pocket Books.

Mulligan, M. (1977). *An investigation of factors associated with violent modes of conflict resolution in the family.* Unpublished master's thesis, University of Rhode Island.

Nagi, S. (1975). Child abuse and neglect programs: A national overview. *Children Today, 4,* 13-17.

National Center on Child Abuse and Neglect. (1988). *Study findings: Study of national incidence and prevalence of child abuse and neglect: 1988.* Washington, DC: U.S. Department of Health and Human Services.

National Center on Child Abuse and Neglect. (1996). *Study findings: Study of national incidence and prevalence of child abuse and neglect: 1993.* Washington, DC: U.S. Department of Health and Human Services.

National Center on Elder Abuse. (1995). *The national elder abuse incidence study.* Unpublished report. Washington, DC. (Mimeographed).

National Opinion Research Center. (1991). *General Social Surveys, 1972-1991 cumulative codebook.* Storrs, CT: Roper Center for Public Opinion Research.

National Research Council. (1993). *Understanding child abuse and neglect.* Washington, DC: National Academy Press.

Neidig, P., Friedman, D., & Collins, B. (1985). Domestic conflict containment: A spouse abuse treatment program. *Social Casework: The Journal of Contemporary Social Work, 66,* 195-204.

Neidig, P., Friedman, D., & Collins, B. (1986). Attitudinal characteristics of males who have engaged in spouse abuse. *Journal of Family Violence, 1,* 223-233.

Nelson, B. J. (1984). *Making an issue of child abuse: Political agenda setting for social problems.* Chicago: University of Chicago Press.

Newberger, E., Reed, R., Daniel, J. H., Hyde, J., & Kotelchuck, M. (1977). Pediatric social illness: Toward an etiologic classification. *Pediatrics, 60,* 178-185.

NiCarthy, G. (1983). Addictive love and abuse: A course for teen-aged women. In S. Davidson (Ed.), *The second mile: Contemporary approaches in counseling young women* (pp. 115-159). Tucson, AZ: New Directions for Women.

Nye, F. I. (1979). Choice, exchange, and the family. In W. R. Burr, R. Hill, F. I. Nye, & I. L. Reiss (Eds.), *Contemporary theories about the family* (Vol. 2, pp. 1-41). New York: Free Press.

O'Brien, J. (1971). Violence in divorce prone families. *Journal of Marriage and the Family, 33,* 692-698.

O'Brien, M. J. (1991). Taking sibling abuse seriously. In M. Patton (Ed.), *Family sexual abuse: Frontline research and evaluation* (pp. 75-92). Newbury Park: CA: Sage.

Ogg, J., & Bennett, G. (1992). Elder abuse in Britain. *British Medical Journal, 305,* 998-999.

O'Leary, K. D. (1988). Physical aggression between spouses: A social learning perspective. In V. B. Van Hasselt, R. L. Morrison, A. S. Bellack, & M. Hersen (Eds.), *Handbook of family violence* (pp. 31-55). New York: Plenum.

O'Sullivan, C., Wise, J., & Douglass, V. (1995, July). *Domestic violence shelter residents in New York City: Profile, needs, and alternatives to shelter*. Paper presented at the 4th International Family Violence Research Conference, Durham, NH.

Owens, D., & Straus, M. A. (1975). Childhood violence and adult approval of violence. *Aggressive Behavior, 1*, 193-211.

Pagelow, M. (1981). *Woman-battering: Victims and their experiences*. Beverly Hills, CA: Sage.

Pagelow, M. (1984). *Family violence*. New York: Praeger.

Pagelow, M. (1989). The incidence and prevalence of criminal abuse of other family members. In L. Ohlin & M. Tonry (Eds.), *Family violence* (pp. 263-313). Chicago: University of Chicago Press.

Parke, R. D., & Collmer, C. W. (1975). Child abuse: An interdisciplinary analysis. In M. Hetherington (Ed.), *Review of child development research* (Vol. 5, pp. 1-102). Chicago: University of Chicago Press.

Parnas, R. (1967). The police response to domestic disturbance. *Wisconsin Law Review, 2*, 914-960.

Pate, A. M., & Hamilton, E. E. (1992). Formal and informal social deterrents to domestic violence: The Dade County Spouse Assault Experiment. *American Sociological Review, 57*, 691-697.

Peek, C., Fisher, J. L., & Kidwell, J. S. (1985). Teenage violence towards parents: A neglected dimension of family violence. *Journal of Marriage and the Family, 47*, 1051-1058.

Pelton, L. (1989). *For reasons of poverty: A critical analysis of the public child welfare system in the United States*. New York: Praeger.

Peters, S. D., Wyatt, G. E., & Finkelhor, D. (1986). Prevalence. In D. Finkelhor (Ed.), *A sourcebook on child sexual abuse* (pp. 15-59). Beverly Hills, CA: Sage.

Phillips, L. R. (1983). Abuse of and neglect of the frail elderly at home: An exploration of theoretical relationships. *Journal of Advanced Nursing, 8*, 379-392.

Pillemer, K. (1985). The dangers of dependency: New findings on domestic violence against the elderly. *Social Problems, 33*, 146-158.

Pillemer, K. (1986). Risk factors in elder abuse: Results from a case-control study. In K. Pillemer & R. Wolf (Eds.), *Elder abuse: Conflict in the family* (pp. 239-263). Dover, MA: Auburn House.

Pillemer, K. (1993). The abused offspring are dependent: Abuse is caused by the deviance and dependency of abusive caretakers. In R. J. Gelles & D. Loseke (Eds.), *Current controversies on family violence* (pp. 237-249). Newbury Park, CA: Sage.

Pillemer, K., & Finkelhor, D. (1988). The prevalence of elder abuse: A random sample survey. *The Gerontologist, 28*, 51-57.

Pillemer, K., & Frankel, S. (1991). Domestic violence against the elderly. In M. I. Rosenberg & M. A. Fenley (Eds.), *Violence in America: A public health approach* (pp. 158-183). New York: Oxford University Press.

Pittman, D., & Handy, W. (1964). Patterns in criminal aggravated assault. *Journal of Criminal Law, Criminology, and Police Science, 55* 462-470.

Pizzey, E. (1974). *Scream quietly or the neighbors will hear.* Harmondsworth, UK: Penguin.

Pleck, E. (1987). *Domestic tyranny: The making of American social policy against family violence from colonial times to the present.* New York: Oxford University Press.

Pleck, E., Pleck, J., Grossman, M., & Bart, P. (1978). The battered data syndrome: A comment on Steinmetz's article. *Victimology, 2,* 680-683.

Podnieks, E. (1992). National survey of abuse of the elderly in Canada. *Journal of Elder Abuse & Neglect, 5,* 5-58.

Pokorny, A. (1965). Human violence: A comparison of homicide, aggravated assault, suicide, and attempted suicide. *Journal of Criminal Law, Criminology, and Police Science, 56,* 488-497.

Polansky, N., Chalmers, M. A., Buttenweiser, E., & Williams, D. P. (1981). *Damaged parents: An anatomy of child neglect.* Chicago: University of Chicago Press.

Polansky, N., Gaudin, J. M., & Kilpatrick, A. (1992). Family radicals. *Children and Youth Services Review, 14,* 19-26.

Police Foundation. (1977). *Domestic violence and the police: Studies in Detroit and Kansas City.* Washington, DC: National Institute of Justice.

Prasad, D. (1994). Dowry-related violence: A content analysis of news in selected newspapers. *Journal of Comparative Family Studies, 25,* 71-89.

Preliminary findings regarding child abuse and neglect [Press release]. (1995, December 7). Washington, DC: Department of Health and Human Services.

Prentky, R. (1990, March). *Sexual violence.* Paper prepared for the Panel on Understanding and Control of Violent Behavior, Washington, DC. Washington, DC: National Research Council.

Prescott, S., & Letko, C. (1977). Battered women: A social psychological perspective. In M. Roy (Ed.), *Battered women: A psychosociological study of domestic violence* (pp. 72-96). New York: Van Nostrand Reinhold.

Prochaska, J. O., Norcross, J. C., & DiClemente, C. C. (1994). *Changing for good: The revolutionary program that explains the six stages of change and teaches you how to free yourself from bad habits.* New York: Morrow.

Radbill, S. (1987). Children in a world of violence: A history of child abuse. In R. Helfer & R. Kempe (Eds.), *The battered child* (4th ed., pp. 3-20). Chicago: University of Chicago Press.

Rathbone-McCuan, E. (1980). Elderly victims of family violence and neglect. *Social Casework, 61,* 296-304.

Renzetti, C. (1992). *Intimate betrayal: Partner abuse in lesbian relationships.* Newbury Park, CA: Sage.

Renzetti, C. (1995). Violence in gay and lesbian relationships. In R. Gelles (Ed.), *Visions 2010: Families & violence, abuse, and neglect* (pp. 6ff.). Minneapolis, MN: National Council on Family Relations.

Riggs, D. S., O'Leary, K. D., & Breslin, F. C. (1990). Multiple predictors of physical aggression in dating couples. *Journal of Interpersonal Violence, 5,* 61-73.

Robin, M. (1982). Historical introduction: Sheltering arms: The roots of child protection. In E. H. Newberger (Ed.), *Child abuse* (pp. 1-41). Boston: Little, Brown.

Rodgers, K. (1994). Wife assault: The findings of a national survey. *Juristate Service Bulletin, 14*, 1-22.

Roscoe, B., & Bernaske, N. (1985). Courtship violence experienced by abused wives: Similarities in patterns of abuse. *Family Relations, 34*, 419-424.

Rosenbaum, A., & O'Leary, K. D. (1981). Marital violence: Characteristics of abusive couples. *Journal of Consulting and Clinical Psychology, 49*, 63-71.

Rosenfeld, A., & Newberger, E. H. (1977). Compassion vs. control: Conceptual and practical pitfalls in the broadened definition of child abuse. *Journal of the American Medical Association, 237*, 2086-2088.

Rosenfeld, B. D. (1992). Court-ordered treatment of spouse abuse. *Clinical Psychology Review, 12*, 205-226.

Rossi, P. (1992). Assessing family preservation program. *Child and Youth Services Review, 14*, 77-97.

Rounsaville, B.J. (1978). Theories of marital violence: Evidence from a study of battered women. *Victimology, 3*, 11-31.

Roy, M. (Ed.). (1977). *Battered women: A psychosociological study of domestic violence.* New York: Van Nostrand Reinhold.

Russell, D. (1980, August). *The prevalence and impact of marital rape in San Francisco.* Paper presented at the annual meeting of the American Sociological Association, New York.

Russell, D. (1984). *Sexual exploitation: Rape, child sexual abuse, and workplace harassment.* Beverly Hills, CA: Sage.

Sack, W. H., Mason, R., & Higgins, J. E. (1985). The single-parent family and abusive child punishment. *American Journal of Orthopsychiatry, 55*, 252-259.

Sargent, D. (1962). Children who kill—A family conspiracy. *Social Work, 7*, 35-42.

Saunders, D. G., & Hanusa, D. (1986). Cognitive-behavioral treatment for men who batter: The short-term effects of group therapy. *Journal of Family Violence, 1*, 357-372.

Schuerman, J., Rzepnicki, T. L., & Littell, J. H. (1994). *Putting families first: An experiment in family preservation.* New York: Aldine de Gruyter.

Sedlak, A. (1988). The use and psychological impact of a battered women's shelter. In G. T. Hotaling, D. Finkelhor, J. T. Kirkpatrick, & M. A. Straus (Eds.), *Coping with family violence: Research and policy perspectives* (pp. 122-128). Newbury Park, CA: Sage.

Shainess, N. (1977). Psychological aspects of wife battering. In M. Roy (Ed.), *Battered women: A psychosociological study of domestic violence* (pp. 111-119). New York: Van Nostrand Reinhold.

Sherman, L. (1992). *Policing domestic violence: Experiments and dilemmas.* New York: Free Press.

Sherman, L., & Berk, R. (1984). The specific deterrent effects of arrest for domestic assault. *American Sociological Review, 49*, 261-272.

Sherman, L. W., & Smith, D. A. (1992). Crime, punishment, and stake in conformity: Legal and informal control of domestic violence. *American Sociological Review, 57*, 680-690.

Sherven, J., & Sniechowski, J. (1994). Women are responsible, too. *Los Angeles Times.*

Simmel, G. (1950). *The sociology of Georg Simmel* (K. Wolf, Ed.). New York: Free Press.

Smith, E. O., & Byrd, L. (1987). External and internal influences on aggression in captive group-living monkeys. In R. Gelles & J. Lancaster (Eds.), *Child abuse and neglect: Biosocial dimensions* (pp. 175-199). Hawthorne, NY: Aldine de Gruyter.

Smith, M. (1991a). Male peer support of wife abuse: An exploratory study. *Journal of Interpersonal Violence, 6*, 512-519.

Smith, M. (1991b). Patriarchal ideology and wife beating: A test of a feminist hypothesis. *Violence and Victims, 5*, 257-273.

Smith, S. (1965). The adolescent murderer. *Archives of General Psychiatry, 13*, 310-319.

Smith, S., Honigsberger, L., & Smith, C. (1973). E.E.G. and personality factors in baby batterers. *British Medical Journal, 2*, 20-22.

Smuts, B. (1992). Male aggression against women: An evolutionary perspective. *Human Nature, 3*, 1-44.

Snell, J. E., Rosenwald, R. J., & Robey, A. (1964). The wifebeater's wife: A study of family interaction. *Archives of General Psychiatry, 11*, 107-113.

Sommers, C. H. (1994). *Who stole feminism? How women have betrayed women*. New York: Simon & Schuster.

Star, B., Clark, C. G., Goetz, K. M., & O'Malia, L. (1979). Psychological aspects of wife battering. *Social Casework, 60*, 479-487.

Stark, E., & Flitcraft, A. (1996). *Women at risk: Domestic violence and women's health*. Thousand Oaks, CA: Sage.

Stark, E., Flitcraft, A., Zuckerman, D., Grey, A., Robison, J., & Frazier, W. (1981). *Wife abuse in the medical setting: An introduction for health personnel*. Monograph No. 7. Washington, DC: Office of Domestic Violence.

Stark, R., & McEvoy, J. (1970). Middle class violence. *Psychology Today, 4*, 52-65.

Starr, R. H., Jr. (1982). A research based approach to the prediction of child abuse. In R. H. Starr, Jr. (Ed.), *Child abuse prediction: Policy implications* (pp. 105-142). Cambridge, MA: Ballinger.

Starr, R. H., Jr. (1988). Physical abuse of children. In V. B. Van Hasselt, R. L. Morrison, A. S. Bellack, & M. Hersen (Eds.), *Handbook of family violence* (pp. 119-155). New York: Plenum.

Steele, B. F. (1978). The child abuser. In I. Kutash, S. B. Kutash, L. B. Schlesinger, & Associates (Eds.), *Violence: Perspectives on murder and aggression* (pp. 285-300). San Francisco: Jossey-Bass.

Steele, B. F., & Pollack, C. (1974). A psychiatric study of parents who abuse infants and small children. In R. Helfer & C. Kempe (Eds.), *The battered child* (2nd ed., pp. 89-134). Chicago: University of Chicago Press.

Steffensmeier, D., Allan, E. A., Harer, M., & Streifel, C. (1989). Age and the distribution of crime. *American Journal of Sociology, 94*, 803-831.

Steinmetz, S. K. (1971). Occupation and physical punishment: A response to Straus. *Journal of Marriage and the Family, 33*, 664-666.

Steinmetz, S. K. (1977). *The cycle of violence: Assertive, aggressive, and abusive family interaction*. New York: Praeger.

Steinmetz, S. K. (1978a). The battered husband syndrome. *Victimology, 2*, 499-509.

Steinmetz, S. K. (1978b). Violence between family members. *Marriage and Family Review, 1*, 1-16.

Steinmetz, S. K. (1978c). Battered parents. *Society, 15,* 54-55.

Steinmetz, S. K. (1982). A cross-cultural comparison of sibling violence. *International Journal of Family Psychiatry, 2,* 337-351.

Steinmetz, S. K. (1993). The abused elderly are dependent: Abuse is caused by the perception of stress associated with providing care. In R. J. Gelles & D. Loseke (Eds.), *Current controversies on family violence* (pp. 222-236). Newbury Park, CA: Sage.

Stets, J. (1990). Verbal and physical aggression in marriage. *Journal of Marriage and the Family, 52,* 501-514.

Straus, M. (1971). Some social antecedents of physical punishment: A linkage theory interpretation. *Journal of Marriage and the Family, 33,* 658-663.

Straus, M., Kaufman Kantor, G., & Moore, D. (1994, August). *Change in cultural norms approving marital violence.* Paper presented at the annual meetings of the American Sociological Association, Los Angeles.

Straus, M. A. (1979). Measuring intrafamily conflict and aggression: The Conflict Tactics Scale (CT). *Journal of Marriage and the Family, 41,* 75-88.

Straus, M. A. (1980). A sociological perspective on the causes of family violence. In M. R. Green (Ed.), *Violence and the family* (pp. 7-31). Boulder, CO: Westview.

Straus, M. A. (1994). *Beating the devil out of them: Corporal punishment in American families.* New York: Lexington Books.

Straus, M. A., & Gelles, R. J. (1986). Societal change and family violence from 1975 to 1985 as revealed by two national surveys. *Journal of Marriage and the Family, 48,* 465-479.

Straus, M. A., & Gelles, R. J. (1988). Violence in American families: How much is there and why does it occur? In E. W. Nunnally, C. Chilman, & F. M. Cox (Eds.), *Troubled relationships* (pp. 141-162). Newbury Park, CA: Sage

Straus, M. A., & Gelles, R. J. (1990). How violent are American families? Estimates from the National Family Violence Resurvey and other studies. In M. A. Straus & R. J. Gelles (Eds.), *Physical violence in American families: Risk factors and adaptations to violence in 8,145 families* (pp. 95-112). New Brunswick, NJ: Transaction Books.

Straus, M. A., Gelles, R. J., & Steinmetz, S. K. (1980). *Behind closed doors: Violence in the American family.* Garden City, NY: Anchor.

Straus, M. A., & Hotaling, G. T. (1979). *The social causes of husband-wife violence.* Minneapolis: University of Minnesota Press.

Straus, M. A., & Kaufman Kantor, G. (1987). Stress and child abuse. In R. Helfer & R. Kempe (Eds.), *The battered child* (4th ed., pp. 42-59). Chicago: University of Chicago Press.

Straus, M. A., & Kaufman Kantor, G. (1992, July). *Change in spouse assault rates from 1975 to 1992: A comparison of three national surveys in the United States.* Paper presented at the 13th World Congress of Sociology, Bielefeld, Germany.

Straus, M. A., & Smith, C. (1990). Violence in Hispanic families in the United States: Incidence rates and structural interpretations. In M. A. Straus & R. J. Gelles (Eds.), *Physical violence in American families: Risk factors and adaptations to violence in 8,145 families* (pp. 341-367). New Brunswick, NJ: Transaction Books.

Straus, M. A., & Sweet, S. (1992). Verbal aggression in couples: Incidence rates and relationships to personal characteristics. *Journal of Marriage and the Family, 54,* 346-357.

Strube, M. J., & Barbour, L. S. (1983). The decision to leave an abusive relationship: Economic dependence and psychological commitment. *Journal of Marriage and the Family, 45,* 785-793.

Study of high risk child abuse and neglect. (1992). Rockville, MD: Westat.

Sugarman, D., & Hotaling, G. T. (1989). Dating violence: Prevalence, context, and risk markers. In M. A. Pirog-Good & J. E. Stets (Eds.), *Violence in dating relationships: Emerging issues* (pp. 3-32). New York: Praeger.

Tatara, T. (1993a). *Characteristics of children in substitute and adoptive care.* Washington, DC: Voluntary Cooperative Information System, American Public Welfare Association.

Tatara, T. (1993b). Understanding the nature and scope of domestic elder abuse with the use of state aggregate data: Summaries of the key findings of a national survey of state APS and aging agencies. *Journal of Elder Abuse & Neglect, 5,* 35-57.

3 deaths trigger debate over child abuse in China. (1992, December 26). *Providence Journal,* p. C-3.

Toby, J. (1966). Violence and the masculine ideal: Some qualitative data. *Annals of the American Academy of Political and Social Science, 364,* 20-27.

Tooley, K. (1977). The young child as victim of sibling attack. *Social Casework, 58,* 25-28.

Truninger, E. (1971). Marital violence: The legal solutions. *Hastings Law Review, 23,* 259-276.

Turbett, J. P., & O'Toole, R. (1980, August). *Physician's recognition of child abuse.* Paper presented at the annual meeting of the American Sociological Association, New York.

United Nations. (1994). *Violence against women in the family.* New York: Author.

U.S. Advisory Board on Child Abuse and Neglect. (1995). *A nation's shame: Fatal child abuse and neglect in the United States.* Washington, DC: U.S. Department of Health and Human Services.

U.S. Bureau of the Census. (1995). *Statistical abstracts of the United States.* Washington, DC: U.S. Department of Commerce.

U.S. Department of Health and Human Services, National Center on Child Abuse and Neglect. (1995). *Child maltreatment 1993: Reports from the states to the National Center on Child Abuse and Neglect.* Washington, DC: Government Printing Office.

U.S. Department of Health and Human Services, National Center on Child Abuse and Neglect. (1996). *Child maltreatment 1994: Reports from the states to the National Center on Child Abuse and Neglect.* Washington, DC: Government Printing Office.

U.S. Department of Justice. (1980). *Intimate victims: A study of violence among friends and relatives.* Washington, DC: Government Printing Office.

U.S. Department of Justice. (1984, September). *Attorney General's Task Force on Family Violence: Final report.* Washington, DC: Author.

U.S. Department of Justice. (1994a). *Domestic violence: Violence between intimates.* Washington: U.S. Department of Justice, Bureau of Justice Statistics.

U.S. Department of Justice. (1994b). *Uniform Crime Reports for the United States, 1993.* Washington, DC: U.S. Department of Justice, Federal Bureau of Investigation.

U.S. Department of Justice. (1995). *Uniform Crime Reports for the United States, 1994.* Washington, DC: U.S. Department of Justice, Federal Bureau of Investigation.

Vesterdal, J. (1977). Handling of child abuse in Denmark. *Child Abuse & Neglect: The International Journal, 1*, 193-198.

Vissing, Y. M., Straus, M. A., Gelles, R. J., & Harrop, J. W. (1991). Verbal aggression by parents and psychosocial problems of children. *Child Abuse & Neglect: The International Journal, 15*, 223-238.

Walker, L. (1979). *The battered woman.* New York: Harper & Row.

Walker, L. (1993). The battered woman syndrome is a psychological consequence of abuse. In R. J. Gelles & D. Loseke (Eds.), *Current controversies on family violence* (pp. 133-153). Newbury Park, CA: Sage.

Warren, C. (1978, April). *Battered parents: Adolescent violence and the family.* Paper presented at the Pacific Sociological Association, Anaheim, CA.

Wauchope, B., & Straus, M. A. (1990). Physical punishment and physical abuse of American children: Incidence rates by age, gender, and occupational status. In M. Straus & R. J. Gelles (Eds.), *Physical violence in American families: Risk factors and adaptations to violence in 8,145 families* (pp. 113-148). New Brunswick, NJ: Transaction Books.

Weise, D., & Daro, D. (1995). *Current trends on child abuse reporting and fatalities: The results of the 1994 fifty state survey.* Chicago: National Committee to Prevent Child Abuse.

Weitzman, J., & Dreen, K. (1982). Wife-beating: A view of the marital dyad. *Social Casework, 63*, 259-265.

Wertham, F. (1972). Battered children and baffled parents. *Bulletin of the New York Academy of Medicine, 48*, 888-898.

Westman, J. C. (1994). *Licensing parents: Can we prevent child abuse and neglect?* New York: Insight Books.

Wexler, R. (1991). *Wounded innocents: The real victims of the war against children.* Buffalo, NY: Prometheus.

Widom, C. S. (1989a). Child abuse, neglect, and violent criminal behavior. *Criminology, 27*, 251-171.

Widom, C. S. (1989b). The cycle of violence. *Science, 244*, 160-166.

Widom, C. S. (1991). Childhood victimization and adolescent problem behaviors. In M. E. Lamb & R. Ketterlinus (Eds.), *Adolescent problem behaviors* (pp. 127-164). New York: Lawrence Erlbaum.

Widom, C. S. (1995). Victims of childhood sexual abuse—Later criminal consequences. In *National Institute of Justice research in brief.* Washington, DC: U.S. Department of Justice, Office of Justice Programs.

Williams, K. (1992). Social sources of marital violence and deterrence: Testing an integrated theory of assaults between partners. *Journal of Marriage and the Family, 54*, 620-629.

Williams, L. (1994). Recall of childhood trauma: A prospective study of women's memories of child sexual abuse. *Journal of Consulting and Clinical Psychology, 62*, 1167-1176.

Wilson, M., & Daly, M. (1987). Risk of maltreatment of children living with stepparents. In R. J. Gelles & J. B. Lancaster (Eds.), *Child abuse and neglect: Biosocial dimensions* (pp. 215-232). Hawthorne, NY: Aldine de Gruyter.

Wilson, M., & Daly, M. (1993). Spousal homicide risk and estrangement. *Violence and Victims, 8*, 3-16.

Wilson, M., Daly, M., & Weghorst, S. J. (1980). Household composition and the risk of child abuse and neglect. *Journal of Biosocial Science, 12*, 333-340.

Wolf, R. (1995). Abuse of the elderly. In R. Gelles (Ed.), *Visions 2010: Families & violence, abuse, and neglect* (pp. 8-10). Minneapolis, MN: National Council on Family Relations.

Wolf, R., Strugnell, C., & Godkin, M. (1982). *Preliminary findings from three model projects on elderly abuse.* Worcester: University of Massachusetts Medical Center, University Center on Aging.

Wolfgang, M. (1958). *Patterns in criminal homicide.* New York: Wiley.

Wolfner, G. (1996). *Family functioning and physical child abuse: Are certain types more prone to abuse?* Unpublished doctoral dissertation, University of Rhode Island.

Woolley, P., & Evans, W. (1955). Significance of skeletal lesions resembling those of traumatic origin. *Journal of the American Medical Association, 158*, 539-543.

Wright, L. (1971). The "sick but slick" syndrome as a personality component for parents of battered children. *Journal of Clinical Psychology, 32*, 41-45.

Yllö, K. (1983). Using a feminist approach in quantitative research. In D. Finkelhor, R. J. Gelles, G. T. Hotaling, & M. A. Straus (Eds.), *The dark side of families: Current family violence research* (pp. 277-288). Beverly Hills, CA: Sage.

Yllö, K. (1988). Political and methodological debates in wife abuse research. In K. Yllö & M. Bograd (Eds.), *Feminist perspectives on wife abuse* (pp. 28-50). Newbury Park, CA: Sage.

Yllö, K. (1993). Through a feminist lens: Gender, power, and violence. In R. Gelles & D. Loseke (Eds.), *Current controversies on family violence* (pp. 47-62). Newbury Park, CA: Sage.

Young, L. (1964). *Wednesday's child: A study of child neglect and abuse.* New York: McGraw-Hill.

Zellman, G. (1990a). Child abuse reporting and failure to report among mandated reporters. *Journal of Interpersonal Violence, 5*, 3-22.

Zellman, G. (1990b). Report decision-making patterns among mandated child abuse reporters. *Child Abuse & Neglect: The International Journal, 14*, 325-336.

NAME INDEX

SUBJECT INDEX

Abusers. *See* Batterers; Treatment
    programs
Abuse. *See* Family violence; *specific*
    type
Abusive violence:
    defined, 15
    estimates of, 47-49, 48 (table), 52
        (figure), 76 (table), 78, 78
        (figure), 100, 111 (table)
Acquaintance rape, 72-73, 94 (n1)
Adolescents:
    abuse of, 44, 49, 56, 68 (n1), 96,
        103-108, 137, 147
    consequences of abuse to, 67
    parent abuse by, 109-111, 111 (table),
        112-113
    sibling violence, 100, 102-103
    See also Courtship violence
Adult protective services. *See* Elder
    abuse
Adults:
    child victims as abusers, 8-9, 62-64, 65
        (figure), 84, 119, 128-129, 138,
        166
    consequences of childhood abuse in,
        67-68
    See also Battered women; Batterers;
        Elder abuse; Parents

African Americans. *See* Blacks
Ages:
    as risk factors in child abuse, 49, 54,
        56, 60, 65 (figure), 105
    in courtship violence, 72
    in marital violence disputes, 82
    of elder abuse victims, 116
    sibling violence, 102-103
    within family structure, 53, 125
Alcohol:
    as disinhibitor, 10-11
    batterers' use of, 82, 156
    child abuse and, 57-58, 67
Amphetamines, violence and use of,
    11
Anger management, 163
Anxiety:
    in abused parents, 109
    in battered women, 81
    in child abusers, 57
Arrests:
    attitudes toward, 38
    mandatory, 138-139, 156-158
Asia:
    child abuse in, 25-26
    marital violence in, 24
Australia, violence against women in,
    22-23

195

ABOUT THE AUTHOR

Richard J. Gelles is Professor of Sociology and Psychology and the Director of the Family Violence Research Program at the University of Rhode Island.

His book *The Violent Home* was the first systematic empirical investigation of family violence and continues to be highly influential. He is author or coauthor of 20 books and more than 100 articles and chapters on family violence. His latest book is *The Book of David: How Preserving Families Can Cost Children's Lives* (1996).

Gelles received his A.B. degree from Bates College (1968), an M.A. in sociology from the University of Rochester (1971), and a Ph.D. in sociology from the University of New Hampshire (1973). He edited the journal *Teaching Sociology* from 1973 to 1981 and received the American Sociological Association, Section on Undergraduate Education, "Outstanding Contributions to Teaching Award" in 1979. Gelles has presented innumerable lectures to policy-making groups and media groups, including "The Today Show," "CBS Morning News," "Good Morning America," "The Oprah Winfrey Show," "Dateline," and "All Things Considered." In 1984, *Esquire* named him one of the men and women who are "changing America."

Presently, Gelles lives in Kingston, Rhode Island with his wife, Judy, a photographer. His son Jason graduated from Harvard University in 1996, and his son David is a sophomore at Tufts University.

DATE DUE

OC 27 '06			
AUG 2 0 2009			
4810			

DEMCO 38-296